# Theories of the Multinational Firm

To Britta

# Theories of the Multinational Firm

A Multidimensional Creature in the Global Economy, Second Edition

Mats Forsgren

*Department of Business Studies, Uppsala University, Sweden*

**Edward Elgar**

Cheltenham, UK • Northampton, MA, USA

Published by
Edward Elgar Publishing Limited
The Lypiatts
15 Lansdown Road
Cheltenham
Glos GL50 2JA
UK

Edward Elgar Publishing, Inc.
William Pratt House
9 Dewey Court
Northampton
Massachusetts 01060
USA

Paperback edition reprinted 2013

A catalogue record for this book
is available from the British Library

Library of Congress Control Number: 2012948162

MIX
Paper from
responsible sources
FSC
www.fsc.org    FSC® C021018

ISBN 978 1 78100 645 0 (cased)
      978 1 78195 817 9 (paperback)

Typeset by Servis Filmsetting Ltd, Stockport, Cheshire
Printed in Great Britain by Berforts Information Press Ltd

# Contents

# Preface to the second edition

The first edition of this book has been used in MBA and PhD courses at universities in different countries since its publication in 2008. The six perspectives on multinationals presented in the book have been easy to grasp for the students and have been fruitful as a starting point for discussions in the classroom about the multinational firm as a phenomenon. I have been offered some valuable feedback from students and colleagues, both at the Department of Business Studies in Uppsala, and elsewhere. In the second edition of the book I have used this feedback, together with my own research during the last four years, in improving the manuscript in some major aspects as well as in numerous details. Considering the former revisions, the most important are the following:

- The empirical section of Chapter 1, called 'The multinational firm in the world economy', has been rewritten, including more recent data about foreign direct investments and multinational firms.
- The discussion on 'The eclectic framework' in Chapter 3 has been extended by a section about the relationship between internalization advantage and location-specific advantage when clustering is introduced as an important aspect of the latter advantage.
- In Chapter 3 a discussion of the concept of the multinational firm as a 'global factory' has been added, including a discussion on how this is related to the internalization advantage of the Coordinating multinational.
- In Chapter 4, which deals with the Knowing multinational, the role of headquarters is discussed in more depth through the use of the concept of 'parenting advantage' picked up from the writings about the knowledge-based view. This revision has had some implications for Table 8.1 and the text in Chapter 8.

*Mats Forsgren*
*Uppsala, June 2012*

# Acknowledgements

This book is a result of more than 20 years of experience as a teacher and researcher in international business. In this work I have had the privilege to work closely with inspiring colleagues and friends. I am greatly indebted to the members of the international business group at the Department of Business Studies at Uppsala University, as well as to my friends at Copenhagen Business School (INT and SMG), the Swedish School of Economics (IIB) and the Swedish School of Economics in Helsinki (Department of Organization and Management). A special thank you goes to Desiree Holm for her great support in connection with the production of a preliminary manuscript of this book, and to Merawi Tezera for his invaluable technical assistance.

I have also had invaluable support from other colleagues and friends. Håkan Pihl has done marvellous work in scrutinizing and commenting upon different parts of the manuscript, which has been of great help in my efforts to make as accurate presentations as possible of the different theories. Grazia Ietto-Gillies has been very supportive and has helped me to relate my work to her own book, *Transnational Corporations and International Production: Concepts, Theories and Effects*. I also want to thank Mo Yamin for being such an inspiring partner in discussion over the years. Our discussions actually triggered me to write this book. Finally I want to thank three anonymous reviewers at Edward Elgar for very constructive comments.

# 1.   The multinational firm: a beauty or a beast?

## INTRODUCTION

A Janus face of our time? A beauty or a beast in the global economy? The economic and political debate on globalization contains many conflicting views on multinational firms. Some people emphasize the 'bright side' in terms of their potential contribution to economic growth and national welfare. Multinational firms are said to be important agents of change and of 'creative destruction'. They increase the competitive pressure on domestic firms. They demonstrate and diffuse new technologies throughout the economy. They are necessary agents for globalization (Eden and Lenway 2001).

Other people emphasize the 'dark side', represented by their negative impacts on environment, labour and human rights. Multinational firms have goals that are directed to maximization of profits. Nation states have goals directed to job creation, tax revenues, regional development and a high and rising standard of living. It is argued that these goals are not compatible. The multinational firms' greater access to mobile resources and their character of being 'footloose' belongs to the story on the 'dark side' (Eden and Lenway op. cit.; Rugman 1993).

Some quotes may illustrate the contrasting views. First some quotes from the 'bright side':

> MNEs are, then, increasingly being evaluated by both home and host countries in terms of their contribution towards upgrading the quality of indigenous resources and capabilities, and advancing long term comparative advantage . . . this change in philosophy is leading to a less adversarial and more symbiotic relationship between many governments and MNEs – much along the style of that which has been adopted by the Japanese and Korean government for the past two decades or so. (Dunning 1993, p. 362)

Most governments are 'now acclaiming foreign direct investments as good news after a period of hostility in the 1970s and early 1980s' (Dunning 1994). This quote reflects a conviction of an overriding, harmonious relationship between multinational firms and governments. Multinational firms are agents for technology development and welfare. Some people see the multinational firm as the main actor in the globalization process which in itself reflects the core meaning of the information society due to its intricate, global network structure. For instance, a well-known writer on globalization and the information society, Castells, states that the multinational firm as a 'network enterprise makes material the culture of the informational, global economy: it transforms signals into commodities by processing knowledge' (Castells 1996, p. 188).

An even more optimistic version of the 'bright side' is mirrored in the following quote:

> By virtue of their numbers, the poor represent a significant latent purchasing power that must be unlocked . . . Research indicates that this poverty penalty is universal, although the magnitude differs by country. The poverty penalty is the result of local monopolies, inadequate access, poor distribution, and strong traditional intermediaries. Large-scale private-sector business can 'unlock this poverty penalty' . . . MNCs [multinational corporations] and large firms have to start from a deep understanding of the nature and the requirements of the BOP[1] . . . and then architect the business models and the management processes around these requirements. This approach to the BOP market will not only allow large firms to succeed in local markets but will also provide the knowledge base to challenge the way they manage the developed markets. (Prahalad 2006, p. 48)

This view reflects a strong belief in the possibility of combining the profit-seeking behaviour of the multinational firms with the needs of the 4 billion people at the bottom of the pyramid. It is claimed that if multinationals realize their potential fortunes that can be exploited in this 'market', the poverty in the world will disappear and the multinational firms will be the main agents for this change.

Other people are sceptical about such a conclusion. They claim, for instance, that there will always be serious conflicts between the multinational firms and the people at the bottom of the pyramid. The following quote is an example of this scepticism:

> The claim for this form of 'inclusive' capitalism seems somewhat of an (ideological) overstatement . . . It primarily applies to MNEs that are not

represented in these locations. The 'market' at the bottom of the pyramid is, in practise, of course already served by the local firms. Where MNEs – with their extremely efficient production methods and deep financial pockets, let alone transfer price methods – focus on this market segment, there is no doubt that they can out-compete local firms. They therefore also 'crowd-out' local firms and local employment, which in the end might generate more poverty than it alleviates. (van Tulder and van der Zwart 2006, p. 268)

An even stronger proponent of the 'dark side' is mirrored in the following:

Such is our legacy. A world in which consumerism is equated with economic policy, where corporate interests reign, where corporations spew their jargon on to the airwaves and stifle nations with their imperial rule. Corporations have become behemoths, huge global giants that wield immense political power . . . fifty-one of the hundred biggest economies in the world are now corporations (twenty-nine out of the top hundred, if measured in value-added terms). The sales of General Motors and Ford are greater than the GDP [gross domestic product] of the whole of sub Saharian Africa; the assets of IBM, BP and General Electric outstrip the economic capabilities of most small nations; Wal-Mart, the supermarket retailer, has higher revenues than most Central and Eastern European states; and Exxon is comparable in economic size to the economies of Chile and Pakistan . . . Business is in the driver's seat, corporations determine the rules of the game, and governments have become referees, enforcing rules laid down by others. (Hertz 2003, pp. 7–8)

Some scholars also question the efficiency of the large multinationals as agents for technological change. For instance: 'It is a widespread perception that the massive corporate giants have become too large and bureaucratic to compete against the more nimble and innovative smaller firms that we are told are rapidly gaining the advantage in highly competitive global markets' (Korten 2001, p. 206).

The quotes above demonstrate totally divergent views on the political and economical role of multinational firms. Are they beasts or beauties? There is no simple answer to that question. But behind a view there is always a theory. Most often the theories are implicit rather than explicit. But they are always there, somewhere. If we discover the theory with its basic assumptions, we can also reach a better understanding of a certain position. We may not agree with the position. But at least we understand better why we do not agree.

This book claims that different theories produce different views on the 'bright side' and the 'dark side' of the multinational firm. For instance, some theories are more 'functionalistic' than other theories. They tend to assume that multinational firms, as firms, are more efficient than other firms, also from a societal point of view. Simply speaking, we have the firms we have because they are the best ones. Other theories are less conditional in that sense. They claim that multinational firms are social agents with their pros and cons. They can be beauties but they can also be beasts.

Theories may also differ substantially in their view on the multinational firm as an organization. Some theories assume that they function as hierarchies over which the top management has full control. Other theories stress the loosely coupled character in which the power is distributed among several subunits. Some theories posit that multinational firms are efficient vehicles for the transfer of knowledge and capabilities across borders. Other theories emphasize the existence of organizational barriers within the multinational firm which limit such knowledge transfer. Some theories claim that multinational firms exist and survive because they are able to adapt their strategy, organization and control systems to changes in the environment. Other theories, on the contrary, argue that the multinational firm has the ability to shape the environment in accordance with its own interest.

Differences between theories largely explain the contradictory views among scholars. The basic building blocks of a theory reveal the reason for a certain position. An important task, therefore, is to make the different theories more explicit. By doing so it becomes easier to understand the view. Sometimes a specific view follows straight and simply from the underlying theory. Sometimes the relationship between theory and a certain statement is more indicative. In both cases, though, it is easier to understand the reason for the specific opinion if the underlying theoretical platform becomes more visible.

In this book six different theoretical approaches to the multinational firm will be presented and analysed. During the last four decades these approaches have dominated the writings on the multinational firm, at least among scholars within the field of international business. But first I will say a few words about the multinational firm as an empirical phenomenon.

# THE MULTINATIONAL FIRM IN THE WORLD ECONOMY

There is no doubt that the multinational firm as a business actor has increased its relative importance in the world economy over the years. At the end of the 1960s there were approximately 7000 registered multinationals (van Tulder and van der Zwart 2006). In the early 1990s the number had increased to approximately 37000 with at least 170000 foreign affiliates. Fifteen years later the number of multinational firms had almost doubled, to 70000, and the number of foreign affiliates had quadrupled (World Investment Report 2005). The increasing importance of the multinational firm is mirrored in the investments made by firms in foreign subsidiaries in relation to world production and export. Table 1.1 shows some selected indicators of foreign direct investment, export and international production, 1990–2010.[2]

*Table 1.1*   *Selected indicators of foreign direct investment (FDI), export and international production 1990–2010 (billions of dollars, current prices)*

| Item | 1990 | 2003 | 2010 |
|---|---|---|---|
| FDI inflows | 207 | 633 | 1244 |
| FDI outflows | 241 | 617 | 1323 |
| FDI inward stock | 2081 | 7997 | 19141 |
| FDI outward stock | 2094 | 8731 | 20408 |
| Cross-border M&As | 99 | 297 | 339 |
| Sales of foreign affiliates | 5105 | 16963 | 32960 |
| Total assets of foreign affiliates | 4602 | 32186 | 56998 |
| Exports of foreign affiliates | 1498 | 3073 | 6239 |
| Employment of foreign affiliates (thousands) | 21470 | 53196 | 68218 |
| World GDP (in current prices) | 22206 | 36327 | 62909 |
| Gross fixed capital formation | 5109 | 7853 | 13940 |
| Royalties and fee receipts | 29 | 93 | 191 |
| World's exports of goods and services | 4382 | 9216 | 18713 |

*Source:* World Investment Report (2005, 2007, 2011).

Between 1990 and 2010 the world's outflow of foreign direct investment increased from 241 billion dollars to 1323 billion dollars, that is, an increase of 450 per cent. The corresponding figure for the world's export is 327 per cent and for the world's production 182 per cent. Behind these figures is a dramatic increase in terms of expansion across country borders by multinational firms. As a result of this expansion the estimated employment in foreign affiliates rose by 217 per cent, the estimated sales by more than 546 per cent, the export by 316 per cent and the total assets by more than 1000 per cent.

The table also reveals that foreign direct investment is largely carried out by one firm buying another firm in a foreign country. The estimated amount of mergers and acquisitions (M&As) across borders is on average about 40 per cent of the total amount of the outflow of foreign direct investment in the world between 1990 and 2010. In the developed countries this figure is often close to 80 per cent (World Investment Report 2000). As foreign direct investment includes retained earnings and intra-company loans, the importance of mergers and acquisitions relative to greenfield investment is even higher. This means that globalization in terms of multinational firms expanding their cross-border activities is a change and expansion in terms of ownership as much as it is in terms of organic growth. To a large extent this also explains why the increase of foreign direct investment is so much higher than the increase in world production.

Who are these multinational firms which gradually have spread their activities in a large number of countries to a larger and larger degree? Where do they come from and how dominating are they today?

Table A.1 in the Appendix contains a list of the 100 largest non-financial multinational firms, ranked by foreign assets. Although the total number of multinational firms is very high, approximately around 70 000, the global scene is dominated by some few, large multinationals. The 100 largest non-financial multinationals account for 13 per cent of the employment of all multinationals in the world (World Investment Report 2011). The ten largest in 2008 ranked by foreign assets were General Electric (electronics), Royal Dutch Shell (petroleum), Vodafone (telecommunications), BP (petroleum), Toyota (motor vehicles), Exxon (petroleum), Total (petroleum), E.ON (energy), Electricité de France energy) and Arcelor Mittal (metal products). On the whole the list of the 100 largest is relatively stable over time. Around 50 per cent of the 100 or the 50 largest multinationals in 1998 also belonged to this group ten years later. Dominating industries on the list are motor vehicles (Toyota, Volkswagen, Ford, Honda, Daimler, BMW, Nissan, Fiat, General Motors, Volvo, Hyundai), electrical and electronic equipment (General Electric, Siemens, Sony, IBM, Nokia, Hewlett-Packard, Philips, Samsung, Hitachi, Matsushita), telecommunication (Vodafone, Telefonica, Deutsche Telecom, France Telecom, Vivendi, Liberty Global, TeliaSonera), energy (Royal Dutch Shell, BP, Exxon, Total, E.ON, Electricité de France, Chevron, ENI Group, ConocoPhillips, Iberdrola, RWE Group, Veolia, Statoil, National Grid Transco, Repsol, Vattenfall, BG Group Plc, Petronas), pharmaceuticals (Roche, Sanofi-aventis, Pfizer, Novartis, Johnson & Johnson, AstraZeneca, GlaxoSmithKline, Bayer, Teva Pharmaceutical) and retail and trade (Wal-Mart, Mitsui, Pinault-Printemp, Metro, Carrefour, Sumitomo, Marubeni). Newcomers on the list compared to ten years earlier are primarily firms within the energy sector (11 firms), metal and non-metallic products (seven firms) and pharmaceuticals (seven firms).

The dominance of large multinationals is also apparent when it comes to geographical concentration where the parent company is located. Table A.1 in the Appendix reveals that the majority of the 100 largest multinationals have their home base in one of five countries, namely the United States (18), France (15), the United Kingdom (UK) (14), Germany (13) and Japan (9). New home countries compared to 1998 are China, Hong Kong China, Mexico, South Korea, Malaysia, Portugal, Norway and Israel.

Other indicators of the size of these firms on the global scene are the number of foreign affiliates and the 'transnationality index'. The overwhelming majority of the 100 largest multinationals in 2006 had more than 150 foreign affiliates, 24 had over 300 foreign affiliates, nine had over 600 and two – General Electric (electronics) and WPP group (business services) – had over 900 foreign affiliates (World Investment Report 2006). The management problems related to these enormously geographically and operationally dispersed structures should not be underestimated.

A company's transnationality index is composed of an average of foreign sales, assets and employment as a percentage of total sales, assets and employment. For the 100 largest multinationals the index is on average 50 per cent, and a quarter of the firms had an index of more than 75 per cent. Some firms, such as Wal-Mart, Mitsubishi, Statoil, Petronas, Marubeni and Hitachi, had almost all of their activities abroad.

Table A.2 in the Appendix contains a list of the 100 largest non-financial multinationals from developing and transition economies in 2008. Asia dominates as home region on the list, with 67 companies, while the rest come from Russia (8) South Africa (8), the Middle East (8), South America (5) and Mexico (4). Seven of these companies were also among the world's 100 largest in 2008: Hutchison (Hong Kong), CITIC Group and China Ocean Shipping (China), Samsung and Hyundai (South Korea) and Petronas (Malaysia). Ten years earlier only one belonged to the list of the 100 largest (Petroleos de Venezuela, rank 91). The number of multinational firms from developing economies has increased over the years, and so have their foreign activities. For instance, during the period 1998–2008 the ten largest multinationals increased their foreign assets by 225 per cent while the corresponding figure for the ten largest multinationals from developing and transitional economies is approximately 700 per cent (World Investment Report 1998, 2008). The increasing dominance of China in the global economy is reflected in that more than a quarter of the 100 largest multinationals from developing and transition economies are firms from China or Hong Kong, of which three also belong to the 100 largest in the world.

It should be pointed out that a relatively high percentage of the largest multinationals are state-owned enterprises, that is, firms in which governments have a controlling interest. In 2010, 19 of the largest 100 multinationals were state-owned enterprises, and among the 100 largest from the developing and transition economies the corresponding figure is 28 (World Investment Report 2011). Examples of firms in the first group are CITIC Group and China Ocean Shipping (China), Volkswagen, Deutsche Telecom and Deutsche Post (Germany), GDF, EDF, France Telecom, EADS, Veolia and Renault (France), Vattenfall (Sweden) and Statoil (Norway).

It is also striking that when it comes to the nationality of the largest multinationals there are still white spots on the world map: Africa (except for South Africa), South America (except for Argentina, Brazil and Venezuela), the Middle East and Eastern Europe. For instance, countries like the Democratic Republic of Congo, with an enormously rich and more or less complete sample card of all kinds

*Table 1.2    The top 20 multinational firms in terms of R&D expenditure and the corresponding figure for all firms in the home country, 2003 (billions of dollars)*

| World rank | Company | R&D expenditure | Home country |
|---|---|---|---|
| 1 | Ford | 6.8 | USA |
| 2 | Pfizer | 6.5 | USA |
| 6 | General Motors | 5.2 | USA |
| 9 | IBM | 4.6 | USA |
| 12 | Johnson & Johnson | 4.3 | USA |
| 13 | Microsoft | 4.2 | USA |
| 14 | Intel | 4.0 | USA |
| 19 | Motorola | 3.4 | USA |
| | | Subtotal: 39.0 | USA expenditure: 276.2 |
| 3 | Daimler Chrysler | 6.4 | Germany |
| 4 | Siemens | 6.3 | Germany |
| 8 | Volkswagen | 4.8 | Germany |
| | | Subtotal: 17.5 | Germany expenditure: 50.2 |
| 5 | Toyota Motors | 5.7 | Japan |
| 7 | Matsushita Electric | 4.9 | Japan |
| 15 | Sony | 3.8 | Japan |
| 16 | Honda Motor | 3.7 | Japan |
| | | Subtotal: 18.1 | Japan expenditure: 133.0 |
| 18 | Roche | 3.5 | Switzerland |
| 20 | Novartis | 3.4 | Switzerland |
| | | Subtotal: 6.9 | Switzerland expenditure: 6.3 |
| 11 | GlaxoSmithKline | 4.6 | UK expenditure: 29.3 |
| 10 | Nokia | 4.6 | Finland expenditure: 4.5 |
| 17 | Ericsson | 3.7 | Sweden expenditure: 9.4 |

*Source:* World Investment Report (2005).

of metal and non-metallic minerals; and Nigeria, with a considerable portion of world's oil reserves, are totally dependent on investments from abroad for the exploitation of these resources.

Another indicator of the relative dominance of the largest multinationals is the spending on research and development (R&D). Table 1.2 includes the 20 multinationals with the largest R&D expenditure and a comparison with the total R&D expenditure in the business sector in their home countries.

The table reveals that the largest R&D spenders also dominate the total spending on R&D in the business sector in the home country. Of the 20 at the top, eight are US firms with a total spending on R&D of $39 billion. This corresponds to 14 per cent of the total R&D spending among firms within the USA. The corresponding figure for Germany and Sweden is even more striking: the expenditure of the three German firms in the top 20 – Daimler Chrysler, Siemens and Volkswagen – corresponds to 35 per cent of the R&D spending in the German business sector. In Sweden, Ericsson's R&D is almost 40 per cent of that in the Swedish business sector. In small countries the large multinationals can even outweigh the total R&D spending within the country. For instance, the total R&D spending in Roche and Novartis is larger than the R&D spending in whole of Switzerland, and the same goes for Nokia in Finland. These figures indicate the dominant position for large multinationals in their own home countries.

## OUTLINE OF THE BOOK

In the following chapters six different perspectives on the multinational firm are presented. They have in common that they: (1) put the multinational firm rather than the country at the centre of the analysis;[3] (2) ground the reasoning in a coherent theory of the firm; and (3) have all been launched during the last four decades.

Chapter 2, 'The Dominating multinational: a tale of market power' presents the first theory on foreign direct investment, developed by the economist Stephen Hymer. It applies industrial organization theory to foreign direct investment and is the first attempt to develop a model at the firm level. It has had a tremendous impact on all later theory development in the field and can be seen as the origin of all modern thinking about multinational firms. Inspired by Hymer's view, but also in opposition to that view, a different model of the multinational firm is presented in Chapter 3, 'The Coordinating multinational: a tale of cost efficiency'. This model is first of all an application of transaction cost economics to the multinational firm. It argues that the existence of multinational firms reflects difficulties in the market in handling certain transactions between independent firms. Multinational firms internalize such transactions and coordinate them across country borders. The theory in Chapter 4, 'The Knowing multinational: a tale of value creation', develops further a basic premise in the former theories: the necessity of a multinational firm to possess a competitive advantage. In contrast to these theories, though, this approach tries to explain the origin and development of the competitive advantage. It argues that the never-ending process of creation of such firm-unique values is an important explanation for the existence and behaviour of multinational firms. This approach is firmly rooted in the so-called resource-based view or knowledge-based view of the firm.

The theories above represent different approaches but are all basically rooted in economic theory. The three following chapters contain theories that get their inspiration from different types of organization theory rather than economic theory.[4] Chapter 5, 'The Designing multinational: a tale of strategic fit', focuses on the multinational firm as an organization in terms of its structure and control systems. The view is that multinational firms can exist in the long run if, and only if, they have the ability to adapt their organization and control system to changes in the environment. In contrast to the former theories, this approach puts the environment of the multinational firm much more at the centre of the analysis. Contingency theory is the basic platform for this analysis. In Chapter 6, 'The Networking multinational: a tale of business relationships', the business environment of the multinational firm plays an even more crucial role. The environment is first of all defined in terms of business relationships with customers, suppliers and other counterparts. This approach claims that the business network, in which each subsidiary is embedded, has a profound impact on the 'internal life' of the multinational firm in terms of decisions about strategies and future investments. Business network theory and resource dependence theory are the foundations for this approach. In Chapter 7, 'The Politicizing multinational: a tale of legitimacy and power', the multinational firm as a political rather than as a business actor is highlighted. This approach focuses on the different institutional environments that the multinational firm has to deal with, but also the possibility of the firm influencing these environments through different means. Its inspiration is institutionalization theory.

Each chapter tries to answer three main questions: What are the basic building blocks of the theory? What is the role of the multinational firm in society, as derived from the theory? How is the multinational firm conceptualized by the theory as an organization?

In Chapter 8, 'The Multidimensional multinational: concluding remarks', the book is summarized by comparing the different approaches along some critical dimensions.

## NOTES

1.  BOP stands for the 'bottom of the pyramid', that, is the 4 billion people who live on less than $2 per day.
2.  Foreign direct investment is an investment made by a company in another country than the home country involving a lasting interest. Foreign direct investment usually includes an equity stake of at least 10 per cent and consists of three components: equity capital, intra-company loans and reinvested earnings.
3.  Examples of theories in which the country rather than the firm is the focus are Vernon's product life cycle model (see Vernon 1966) and Aliber's model of foreign direct investment (see Aliber 1970).
4.  It is difficult, and maybe not meaningful, to make a sharp distinction between economic theory and organization theory. In this context it is enough to say that organization theory tends to put more focus on the 'internal life' of the multinational firm than does economic theory.

# 2. The Dominating multinational: a tale of market power

## INTRODUCTION

During the 1960s a dramatic shift occurred in how we perceive the multinational firm. Prior to that, firms' investments abroad were seen simply as international capital movements. It was primarily a phenomenon at the macro level. The firm as an organization was not assigned a specific role in the theories that explained why financial capital moved from one country to another. No distinction was made between capital movements in terms of the purchase of stocks, bonds or short-term credits, and capital movements linked to a firm's decision to invest in foreign countries through the establishment of affiliates of different kinds.

By the 1960s, this oversight had become rather inconvenient. In the USA, in particular, it became apparent that firms establishing their own operations overseas, which came to be labelled foreign direct investments, had become a large and growing proportion of capital movement from the USA to other countries. This phenomenon led to some important issues being raised on the political agenda. For instance, plagued by a balance-of-payments deficit, largely due to the high expenditure on the Vietnam War, in 1965 the United States imposed a set of voluntary controls on firms' foreign investments. Three years later these controls became mandatory restrictions (Kindleberger 1969). An office concerned with foreign direct investment was established at the US Department of Commerce (hereafter 'the Office') to ensure that these restrictions were imposed. Requests from companies to make investments overseas were judged in terms of their effect on the balance of payments. One immediate problem for the Office, though, was to evaluate the short-term negative impact on the balance of payments against possible positive long-term effects. Firms argued that the investments were motivated by their need to survive and expand in the foreign market. It was expected that dividends and induced exports would later result in a flow of capital back to the USA.

The very existence of the Office not only reflects the political importance of foreign investment, but it also indicates the complexity of analysing this phenomenon. No theory existed that could explain what the long-term consequences would be. Furthermore, which firms were investing abroad, and even more importantly, why, was unknown at that time. The Office needed to determine on what grounds these companies were able to invest, and what their basic motives were.

Of similar concern was the impact of foreign direct investment on employment. Amongst trade unions, for example, apprehension arose about work and employment being 'moved abroad' as a result of foreign investments. Opinions on this issue, though, diverged considerably. For instance, numerical estimations of the impact of foreign direct investments on employment by the US Tariff Commission claimed that American investment abroad had wiped out as many as 1.3 million US jobs by 1973. A calculation from a Harvard Business School study, though, estimated that the same amount of foreign investment had actually created 600 000 jobs (Frank and Freeman 1978). Above all, the divergence reflects the well-known problem in social science of assessing what would have happened had the phenomenon not occurred. In this particular case, the issue becomes one of whether investing in the home country in combination with exporting to the foreign markets would have been a realistic alternative for the firms. Or were foreign direct investments first of all means to protect foreign markets that otherwise would have been lost?

Like the balance-of-payments issue, there was no coherent theory that could be applied to the employment issue, and it became obvious that an answer to the question about the economic impact of foreign direct investment had to be found at the firm level rather than the macro level. Thus, the underlying motive for these investments and the alternatives available needed to be analysed as a question of firms' strategies. This, in turn, reflects the position of each firm in the relevant market context, including the firm's competitive strength vis-à-vis its competitors at home and abroad. As these variables vary between firms and industries, a model that explains foreign direct investments and their economic and social consequences must include firm-specific factors.

At the beginning of the 1960s, the dominant explanation for international capital movements, often called 'portfolio theory', was the following: capital movements in and out of countries occur in response to the interest rates prevailing in the countries in question (Cohen et al. 1979). The interest rates were presumed to vary in response to the differences in the factor endowment ratios of labour and capital. When capital moves from low-interest to high-interest countries, the market approaches equilibrium (Ohlin 1967 [1933]). With perfect international capital markets, there would be one worldwide interest rate, but because the risk of default varies, each country requires a different risk premium (Kindleberger 1973). Consequently, there will always be opportunities for higher returns to be obtained by moving capital from a low-interest country to a high-interest one.

It became increasingly obvious that portfolio theory could not produce a satisfactory explanation for a growing part of the foreign investments that occurred. There were several reasons for this. Portfolio theory predicts that capital movements across borders reflect interest differentials between countries. Although elegant and simple, it could not explain why there was such a high degree of cross-border direct investment. US firms invested heavily abroad, but that did not mean that there was no inflow of capital to the USA. On the contrary, many European firms also invested in the US market. For instance, in 1974, the Swedish household appliance manufacturer Electrolux acquired the US firm Nation Union Electric, with the result that the company's market share for vacuum cleaners in the US market immediately increased from 0 to 25 per cent. This investment could not be explained by the interest differential between Sweden and the USA because, at the same time, the US firm ITT acquired the Swedish company Flygt, a manufacturer of submersible pumps (SOU 1981, p. 43). Evidently investments were being made for reasons other than the possibility of earning higher interest on capital than in the home country

It was also obvious that the extent of foreign direct investment was much higher in certain industries than in others. There seemed to be certain characteristics at the firm and industry level that had an impact on foreign direct investment. Portfolio theory could offer no explanation for this pattern, because it predicts that an interest rate differential would be profitable for all types of firms and industries to exploit. Furthermore, it was apparent that investors often failed to take money with them when they went abroad to invest, borrowing, instead, in the local market (Kindleberger 1969). That is, not all foreign direct investments were equivalent to cross-border capital movements.

Finally, and maybe more importantly, portfolio theory did not say anything about the need for control to be maintained to ensure a return on the capital invested. Why firms had decided to take an awkward route to establish and run the operations in the host country themselves needed an explanation. Why was it so important to obtain control and not only to earn a return? After all, controlling an operation is costly, time-consuming and the outcome is far from certain, especially as it takes place in a foreign country at a distance. Or, expressed otherwise, there must be something linked to these investments that more than counterbalanced the costs. There was an apparent gap between the dominant theory and the real world. Someone needed to address this.

## MARKET POWER OF THE MULTINATIONAL FIRM

It was the Canadian economist Stephen Hymer who stepped in to address the gap between the theory and business practice. He did so in a doctoral thesis submitted at MIT in 1960. The thesis was not published as a book, however, until 1976 (Hymer 1976).[1]

Nowadays, the common view of international business researchers is that Hymer's thesis was a path-breaking achievement that triggered the development of a more comprehensive theory on foreign direct investment. It broke with the traditional view of perceiving foreign direct investment as a phenomenon that could be explained at the macro level. The title of his thesis, 'The international operations of national firms: a study of foreign direct investment', indicates that his focus was the firm and its operations abroad, rather than capital movements across borders. Hymer's thesis was an attempt to formulate a theory of the firm in which the firm's strategic investments abroad were at the very centre of the analysis. Although the thesis did not become widely known until 1976 when it was published, the main building blocks of his theory were introduced during the 1960s by Charles Kindleberger (Kindleberger 1969).

What, then, are the main thoughts in Hymer's model? If we are to understand this, we have to start with the basic research question that triggered its development. This is quite simple: How is it that firms can establish and run a business operation in a host country in competition with local firms in a situation where the foreign investors suffer from a lack of knowledge of how to do business in that country? This lack of knowledge, which came to be labelled the 'liability of foreignness', is an obvious disadvantage to the foreign firm. In a world of perfect competition, we would expect no, or at most very limited, foreign direct investment. If all firms have access to similar resources and technology and the only difference is the liability of foreignness, there would be no possibility of the foreign firm competing with local firms. Why, then, are foreign direct investments not only extensive, but also growing?

Hymer drew the obvious conclusion that a firm that invests abroad must have some kind of advantage strong enough to overcome this disadvantage. Or, in Kindleberger's words, 'In addition to earning more abroad than at home, the investing firm must be able to earn a higher return in the market where it is investing than local firms earn' (Kindleberger 1969, p. 12). So this was the first crucial step: to analyse foreign direct investment at the firm level and, in principle, at the level of the individual firm.

The next step was to formulate a theory for the existence of such firm-specific advantages. How is it that certain firms possess abilities that others do not possess? And how do these abilities arise? As an educated economist, it was natural for Hymer to turn his attention to theories about deviation from pure competition. After all, such deviations imply that some firms control something that is not accessible to all firms, except in a very long-term perspective. The theory of foreign direct investment, therefore, became a theory of market imperfection. That is, some markets are imperfect, because some firms operating in these markets can utilize resources that others cannot. The competition is limited.

Hymer called these resources 'firms' special advantages' (Hymer 1976, p. 33). Firms invest abroad because they want to grow and earn a higher return, and the firms' special advantages provide the platform from which they can do this. In his thesis, the focus was the national firm, which goes abroad and becomes international. The special advantages are, therefore, things that are created and developed in the home market. These advantages are reflected in different

degrees of market imperfection in different industries, and among
groups of firms within one and the same industry.

Hymer did not examine in any detail the kinds of advantages that
firms may use to operate internationally (Yamin 1991). He just noted
that 'there are as many kinds of advantages as there are functions in
making and selling a product' (Hymer 1976, p. 41). Kindleberger,
based on Hymer's reasoning, made a list of what he called monopolistic advantages that produce foreign direct investments:

1.  departure from perfect competition in the goods market, includ-
    ing product differentiation, special marketing skills, retail price
    maintenance, administrated pricing and so forth;
2.  departure from perfect competition in factor markets, including
    the existence of patented or unavailable technology, discrimina-
    tion in access to capital, differences in skills of managers organ-
    ized into firms rather than hired in competitive markets;
3.  internal and external economies of scale, the latter being taken
    advantage of by vertical integration;
4.  government restrictions on output or entry. (Kindleberger 1969,
    p. 14)

As seen above, the reason for market imperfections can take many
forms. Some of them seem to be most closely associated with an
individual firm's own capability development, for example patents
it holds or managers' skills. Other advantages seem to come from
outside the organization, for example concessions from governments
(point 4). In his analysis, Hymer was influenced by the so-called
'industrial organization theory' that had been launched during the
1950s (Bain 1956). This theory was developed as a result of the
discussion of the economic welfare implications of concentration
in industries and the need for a policy against trust buildings. In
the industrial organization theory, concepts such as market concentration (the number of firms in an industry and the distribution
of market shares) and barriers to entry (how difficult it is for newcomers to enter the market), represent important tools for analysing the degree of deviation from perfect competition. Similar to
mainstream thought in this theory, it was Hymer's view that market
concentration and barriers to entry could have a negative impact on
the welfare of society. In that sense, foreign investment was, or at
least could be, damaging to overall economic welfare, as it was by its

nature a demonstration of market power through the exploitation of different forms of monopolistic advantage. In Hymer's thesis, obtaining power through market imperfections created in the home market was a prerequisite for the firm's ability to invest abroad and to become a multinational firm. In his later writing he also proposed that foreign investment by multinational firms actually created more market imperfection (more about this below).

Hymer claimed that the sources of a firm's special advantages could be of many different kinds. Although inspired by his analysis of foreign direct investment, other researchers have tended to focus on a narrow set of firm-specific advantages, often labelled 'intangible assets'. 'Intangible' means that the assets are closely linked to the individual firm's specific skill and, therefore, are hard for other firms to imitate. This view can be illustrated by the following passage from a book by one of these researchers, Richard Caves:

> This intangible asset might take the specific form of a patented process or design, or it might simply rest on know-how shared among employees of the firm. Or the intangible might take the form of a marketing asset. The firm may possess special skills in styling or promoting its product that make it such that the buyer can distinguish it from those of competitors. Such an asset has a revenue productivity for the firm because it signifies the willingness of some buyers to pay more for that firm's product than for an otherwise comparable variety of the same good that lacks this particular touch. Assets of this type are closely akin to product differentiation, a market condition in which the distinctive features of various sellers' outputs cause each competing firm to face its own downward sloping demand curve. Once again, the intangible asset may take the form of a specific property – a registered trademark or brand – or it may rest in marketing and selling skills shared among the firm's employees. Finally, the distinctiveness of the firm's marketing-oriented assets may rest with the firm's ability to come up with frequent innovations; its intangible asset then may be a patented novelty, or simply some new combination of attributes that its rivals cannot quickly or effectively imitate. (Caves 1982, p. 4)

The quote above indicates an important shift in the way that the sources of firm-specific advantages were conceptualized by Caves and some of his followers compared to Hymer's original perspective. For Hymer, the essence of the advantages was rooted in the fact that certain firms are in a situation that deviates from one of pure competition. In that sense, the ability of a firm to invest abroad is based on something that involves at least a slight risk of a negative impact

on the economic welfare of society. Similar to industrial organization theorists, his concern was the fact that market imperfections are
linked to above-normal profits being made by firms which possess
these firm-specific advantages.

In the view adopted by Caves, the firm-specific advantages are
primarily intangible assets created by the firm itself. The advantage
is 'earned' by the firm through its ability to 'come up with frequent
innovations'. This phenomenon will certainly produce a state of
market imperfection through product differentiation. However,
while Hymer was already inclined to deal with it in his thesis as a
(potential) negative factor from a societal point of view (and to take
a stronger stance on this in his writing after 1960), his followers
were more inclined to look upon the phenomenon as a natural consequence of all business life. Some firms are more innovative than
others, and it is these innovative ones that are able to go abroad.
Caves's view implies that the fact that we have multinational firms
reflects the ability of these firms to innovate and demonstrate their
uniqueness. In principle, this view leaves limited room for questioning the welfare implications of the multinational firm, especially if
innovativeness is perceived as fundamental for economic development. Expressed differently, Hymer's concern, rooted in industrial
organization theory, was substituted by a more apolitical view of
firm-specific advantages.

Although Hymer was not very precise in his analysis of the content
of firm-specific advantages, it is obvious that he also included other
reasons for market imperfection than a firm's own innovativeness,
such as discrimination in terms of the access to capital or other
resources, economies of scale, concessions received from governments, and so on. In a certain situation some firms possess advantages that others do not, but the reasons for this can be manifold
and they do not only rest on an ability to innovate new products
or to recombine resources. Other reasons, for instance, can be the
advantage of being the first to make the move, political smartness or
just plain luck. In that sense, Hymer's view of market imperfections
has more to do with the structure in an industry or among a certain
group of firms than a natural condition. His view also implies that
multinational firms can earn high profits and have access to large
amounts of capital over long periods of time without being cost
efficient. Their edge comes from having market power. This market
power can occasionally lead to a state of 'saturation' and 'below-

normal' levels of innovativeness in multinationals, which is quite the opposite to Caves's opinion on what firm-specific advantages are all about.

## HYMER'S VIEW ON THE SOCIETAL ROLE OF THE MULTINATIONAL FIRM

Hymer's proposition that firm-specific advantages are necessary conditions for foreign direct investment had a great impact on other economists' thought. However, as the discussion above demonstrates, the interpretation of what the advantage really is and how it evolves took a somewhat different route from Hymer's original thoughts on the subject. This route led, eventually, to the development of a perspective on multinational firms which is basically much more functionalistic and much less critical than that proposed by Hymer (more about this in Chapter 3).

In writing his thesis, Hymer's main interest was in explaining the initial start of international operations rather than the growth of the multinational firm (Yamin 1991). In his later writing, though, his main concern was the multinational firm as an economic agent in the world economy. It is important, though, to point out that in his thesis he focused on two different factors behind foreign direct investment.[2] The first of these was the possession of particular advantages by firms and the second was 'removal of conflicts' among firms (Yamin *op. cit.*). The first factor came to be what the majority of economists thought of as Hymer's main contribution. The second factor, for different reasons, was hardly noticed or was made short work of. Or, as one economist put it, the point concerning the removal of conflict is 'little more than a distraction' (Teece 2006).

A closer look at Hymer's thesis, though, reveals that one of the most significant aspects of his analysis was that the firms that are active in different countries are connected to each other through their markets. Thereby, they are acting as competitors, which implies that if one firm could control the different enterprises, the joint profit would be increased. This lies at the heart of the idea of the 'removal of conflict' as a driver of foreign direct investment. In particular, if there is a duopolistic or oligopolistic interdependence between the firms, some form of collusion will increase joint profits. Mergers, acquisitions and different types of strategic alliances between firms across borders can be examples of such collusion. The point is that it is not necessary for one of the firms to possess an advantage over the others, although they are likely to be leading members of their respective national oligopolies. The only comparison is whether the increased profit from collusion is more than sufficient to offset the costs of international operations. The important point is that 'international operation is no longer synonymous with the exploitation of some form of firm-specific asset under the firm's own control' (Yamin 1991, p. 68). Yamin also points out that the cases of international operations that Hymer discusses in his thesis belong to the category of 'the removal of conflict', rather than to the 'possession of firm-special advantage'.[3]

Later, in the publications after his thesis, Hymer switched the emphasis of his concern so that the power of multinational firms in the world economy became his dominant theme. It was the actions of these firms that became the primary issue, rather than why and how they had become multinational in the first place. He argued that multinational firms are 'islands of conscious power in an ocean of unconscious cooperation' (Hymer 1970, p. 441). It was their size and their position in the world economy that bothered him. He argued that, while national firms operate under the rights granted by a sovereign state, the multinational firm 'is a social and political (power) structure that organizes large numbers of people, as employees, customers, suppliers, consultants, brokers, counsellors, etc. The large corporation does not operate under the state but alongside it and in some cases above it' (Hymer 1971, p. 140).

Hymer argued that such powerful enterprises as multinationals cannot be analysed by economics alone. But as an educated economist, his arguments rest basically on economics (Buckley 2006). His primary concern was that there are no obvious external correctives to the powerful MNC. In contrast to the 'usual' market in which, in the long run, no firm can violate the system and extract benefits at the expense of other agents, there is no guarantee that this will not happen in a situation where the players are powerful multinationals. By definition, the holder of such power can force other agents, including governments, to act in accordance with partial interests of the firm rather than of the society in which it is operating. In that sense, he trusted Adam Smith's 'invisible hand' and distrusted the 'visible hand' of the large corporations. Through the multinational firm extending its operations to encompass several countries, often through acquisition of local firms or through mergers, the number of independent competitors is reduced. In Hymer's view, then, imperfect markets, which triggered and were a necessary condition for the establishment of the multinational firm in the first place, will be even more imperfect through the firm's continued expansion. For Hymer this was a potential threat to the economic welfare of society.

Hymer's original intention had been to explain why it was possible for foreign direct investment to occur. He found a reasonable answer in industrial organization theory (Cantwell 1991). Firm-specific advantages, manifested in market imperfections, were the platform that national corporations could use to become international. Or, expressed otherwise, local market power triggered internationalization and the establishment of the multinational firm. In the next step he focused on the political and economic power of the multinational firm and the consequences of this power for the world economy at large.

His concern that multinationals reduced the competition in the world market did not prevent him from acknowledging the dual character of foreign direct investment: on one hand as an instrument for transferring capital, technology and organizational skill across borders; and on the other as an instrument for restraining competition between firms in different nations (Hymer 1970). From this point of view, his feelings for multinationals were mixed. He was impressed by their skill in organizing extensive resources and at coordinating activities within one and the same hierarchy. On the other hand, his concern was that the market and society have a limited possibility of controlling what the multinationals are actually doing. They are footloose and beyond the legal control of any national jurisdiction.

He was also fully aware of the fact that market imperfection can be viewed from two perspectives. The first of these is that deviations from full competition interfere with the optimal allocation and efficient use of resources in society. Firms with market power will always limit their production and earn above-normal profits. The second perspective is that a certain degree of market imperfection is a necessary or at least a contributing factor to innovations in the economy. It allows the innovators to capture some of the benefits of their discoveries and thus provide the incentive for research and development (Hymer 1970). Some economists are more inclined to stress the positive consequences of market imperfections on innovation than the negative consequences on (static) optimal resource allocation (Teece 2006).

Hymer recognized that both aspects were valid. However, he was quite specific on two points. Firstly, existing theory does not offer a satisfactory answer to the matter of the level at which the negative implications of market imperfections outweigh the positive consequences. It is quite possible that a large multinational is too powerful in relation to other economic actors, reflected in large accumulated resources and excessive profits, even though some of the company's resources will be ploughed back into innovation. Or in his own words: 'To equate multinational firms' growth with technology and scientific development in general is mystification. In many ways, corporations can frustrate the development potential because that would interfere with their own existence' (Hymer 1971, p. 153). Secondly, even though one cannot question the fact that market imperfections seem to produce a rapid rate of technological change and product innovation (maybe sometimes too rapid), the question is rather the direction of change than the rate of change (Hymer 1970). On this point, Hymer's analysis touches upon the difficult question of the extent to which market forces compel firms to innovate what the consumers want. Or, to put it the other way around, he was concerned that, sooner or later, consumers are forced to buy what the firm has actually innovated. Hymer's fear was that multinationals (and at the time of Hymer's analysis, this primarily concerned US multinationals) direct their efforts to developing products for wealthier groups of consumers, leaving poor people in underdeveloped countries to their destiny.

## HYMER'S VIEW REFLECTED IN COMPETITION POLICY

Although it can be argued that market imperfection is a necessary requirement for innovation and dynamism in an economy, it is obvious that reduced competition is of political concern. Evidence from the Organisation for Economic Co-operation and Development (OECD) indicates that international mergers and acquisitions increased sixfold over the period 1991–98. There was also a fivefold increase in the number of international strategic alliances over the same period (Johnson and Turner 2003). On a national level, different types of competition laws are common. By the end of the twentieth century, more than 80 countries had active competition policies, although around 60 per cent of them had only introduced them since the 1990s (Johnson and Turner *op. cit.*). Foreign direct investment and the globalization of business create special problems for the enforcement of competition law at the national level. The OECD has listed the following three areas of concern in relation to cross-border agreements:

- Cross-border mergers and acquisions: these potentially result in the creation of a monopoly or in the adoption of anti-competitive positions that are under the jurisdiction of more that one competition authority.
- International cartels: joint action by corporations from more than one country under which they agree to divide markets, set prices or divide up bids for projects.
- Strategic business alliances: agreements between competing firms – for example, to develop products or undertake research (Johnson and Turner *op. cit.*).

The first two clearly echo Hymer's view of the impact of foreign direct investment on competition. The key challenge is that the law acts on a national level while business is increasingly international. An increasing need for international agreements and for coordination of national jurisdictions occurs to counteract the power of multinational firms across markets.

There is, though a classical dilemma concerning competition and competition policy in an international context. Within one country, optimal competition policy calls for competitive markets, meaning markets encompassing a sufficient number of producers to prevent any firm from earning above-normal profits. But when maximizing national income from international operations, it can be argued that the nation should extract as much monopoly rent as possible from foreign markets (Caves 1996). From a nation's point of view, therefore, the need for a competition policy differs depending on whether it is the competition within or between markets (countries) that is being considered. In the international arena, the interests firms have in achieving stronger market positions and in decreasing competition by various means may coincide with the home nation's interest.

But this is not the case within the home country's own market (Forsgren 2002).

This dilemma can be illustrated by the discussion that followed the European Union (EU) Commission's decision not to approve Volvo's application to buy Scania. The EU Commission referred to the high market share value in Sweden and the other Nordic countries resulting from this acquisition, while Volvo and the Swedish government referred to the common need of the two companies for a stronger position in the global market. The Swedish government was prepared to sacrifice competition in the home market for the prospect of a Swedish-based company attaining a higher degree of market power abroad and the possibility of earning monopoly rents. The EU Commission had a different view on this matter (Forsgren *op. cit.*).

## WHAT DOES HYMER'S MULTINATIONAL FIRM LOOK LIKE?

'In the giant corporation of today, managers rule from the tops of skyscrapers; on a clear day, they can almost see the world' (Hymer 1970, p. 445). This quotation illustrates how extensive Hymer felt the power of the modern multinational company to be. But how did Hymer perceive multinationals as organizations?

Hymer considered multinational firms to be 'islands of power in an ocean of unconscious cooperation' in which the division of labour between independent firms is substituted by division of labour inside the firm. His theory of foreign direct investment includes a relatively precise view of the multinational firm as an organization. As the quote above indicates, he had no doubts about who governs the multinational firm. The multinational firm is a distinctive hierarchy in which the corporate headquarters decides upon and implements the overall strategies, which are then implemented by the lower levels. He argues that since the beginning of the industrial revolution there has been a steady increase in the size of manufacturing firms, which has been so persistent that it might almost be formulated as a general law of capital accumulation.

In line with Chandler (1962), he identifies three main stages in the development of corporations: from the small, local, enterprise confined to a single function and a single industry, to the multidivisional, international corporation with a highly elaborate admin-istrative structure for organizing the many disparate units with the national corporation between these two extremes (Hymer 1970). The control problem in the giant enterprise is handled by the differentia-tion of management into three levels. The lowest level is concerned with day-to-day operations on the shop floor; the middle level is responsible for coordinating the managers at the lowest level; and the highest level deals with strategy and long-term planning. The basic idea is that the information and decision-making overload at the highest level – a classical problem in the large firms – is handled by separating, completely, the corporate headquarters' function from the levels below it. Thereby, the function of the corporate head-quarters is strategy alone, and not the management of operational or tactical issues.

Although control is maintained by decentralization in the multidi-visional organization, Hymer did not question the assumption that the corporate headquarters had the ultimate decision-making power and was able to pursue the interest of the corporation in whatever manner it chose. He argued that the hierarchy had a dual character:

> In part (hierarchy) fulfils functions of coordination and unification which are necessary wherever larger numbers of units cooperate; in part it fulfils functions that arise from the alienated nature of work in capitalist production . . . The twofold character of the techno-structure is reflected by the twofold nature of the division of labor, which is par-tially based on the greater productivity that results from specialization and partially stems from the principle of divide and rule. The corporate hierarchy is essentially a structure to control the flow of information. It has strong vertical linkages so that information passes up and orders pass down easily, and it has a strong lateral communication at the top in order to obtain concerted action. At the bottom, lateral communication is broken so that the majority cannot consolidate against the minority. (Hymer 1972, p. 102)

'Divide and rule' is a crucial element in Hymer's perception of the multinational firm as an organization. It simultaneously strengthens the lateral communication at the top while breaking it at lower levels to 'prevent alliances and interactions that lead to actions counter to those prescribed by higher management' (Cohen et al. 1979, p. 155). He envisaged that the threat to the top management's monopoly over strategy comes from alliances between different subunits. Consequently, he posited that these subunits were separated from each other in terms of communication, while at the same time communication between different managers at the top level was stimulated as much as possible. This structure will facilitate the 'social power' executed by the top management in the multinational corporation.

His apprehension of the multinational firm as a hierarchy also had consequences on how he considered that they were structured geographically. He argued that the location of the different activities of the multinational firm reflected its hierarchical structure. Owing to the importance of face-to-face contacts within the top management, the corporate headquarters were located in cities such as New York, London, Paris, Tokyo, Frankfurt or Beijing because the headquarters could see 'the whole world' from there. The subunits at the middle level (comprised of the divisional headquarters and the regional headquarters) were located in smaller cities in several countries, while the operational level was spread over many small places in an even larger number of countries. He also presumed that the structure of income and compensation would tend to parallel the structure of status and hierarchy:

> The citizens of capital cities will have the best jobs – allocating men and money at the highest level and planning growth and development – and will receive the highest rates of remuneration . . . The citizens of capital cities will also be the first to innovate new products . . . A new product is usually first introduced to a select group of people who have 'discretionary' income and are willing to experiment in their consumption patterns. (Hymer 1971, p. 123)

In contrast, people on the geographic periphery of the multinational firm have much lower income and remuneration, and they also have a very limited influence on the product development process and the resulting consumption pattern. This is essentially encapsulated by the content of Hymer's 'law of uneven development'.

Hymer's analysis implies that the group residing at the top of the multinational firm would display a strong intolerance towards giving away power to subunits. Furthermore, protecting the interests of the powerful group becomes viable as an important factor in promoting or resisting organizational change. Even though he did not address this issue in particular, the whole tenor of Hymer's analysis suggests that the retention of control over corporate strategy would be the overriding principle determining the extent of multinationality

(Yamin and Forsgren 2006). Or, expressed in a different way, the multinational firm will globalize only to the extent that it will not be detrimental to the corporate headquarters' possibility of retaining full control over the organization. This is maybe one explanation why truly global multinationals – that is, firms that have operations in all of the big continents – are quite rare (Rugman 2003).

## SUMMARY

The development of a modern theory of the multinational firm took off in 1960, when Stephen Hymer wrote his PhD thesis, *The International Operations of National Firms* (Hymer 1976). He showed that portfolio theory could not adequately explain why such a large portion of international investments involved control of the foreign operation, and not only a struggle to earn a higher return on capital. A theory of foreign direct investment was born.

Hymer argued that firms choosing to invest abroad must possess some type of firm-specific advantages that are large enough to outweigh the disadvantages a foreign investor has compared to host-country firms. Otherwise there would be no investments. He addressed the question of what constitutes these advantages. Being an economist he found the answer in industrial organization theory. Firm-specific advantages reflect deviations from perfect competition, that is, market imperfection. Market imperfection offers some firms the ability to exploit an asset in a more profitable way than others (that is, than host-country firms). This ability constitutes both a prerequisite for foreign direct investment and a trigger for such investments, as firms want to grow and earn more money by expanding to new markets.

Although development of a firm-specific advantage includes some element of innovation and is, therefore, valuable for society as a whole, Hymer's perception of the multinational firm as an organization includes some concern about the possible negative impact of market imperfection on social welfare. Even at the time when he wrote his thesis, he included a discussion of the 'removal of conflicts' as a parallel driver of foreign direct investment. He pointed out that international competitors could increase their joint profit through different types of collusion across borders, including mergers, acquisitions, alliances, cartels, and so on.

This issue became more dominant in his later writing, where he stressed the threat that existed from multinational firms exercising market power, and the above-normal profits that accrue to them as a result of this power. His idea of the necessity of a firm-specific advantage has been considered to be much more important than the removal of conflict for most of those involved in the further development of foreign direct investment theory (more on this in Chapters 3 and 4). However, some of his concern is reflected in the present ambition to apply a competition policy on a national and international level as a measure to counterbalance the cross-border activities of multinational firms.

Hymer's perception of the multinational firm as an organization is quite straightforward. He considered the multinational firm to be a clear hierarchy in which the corporate headquarters decides and implements the overall strategies, which are carried out by lower levels. The organization is essentially a structure enabling the top management to control the flow of information. This structure implies strong vertical linkages so that information passes up and orders pass down easily. Lateral communication is something that occurs at the top in order to obtain concerted action at that level. At the bottom, lateral communication is discouraged so that 'the majority cannot consolidate against the minority' (Hymer 1972, p. 102). This is the basic idea behind the 'divide and rule' principle that dominates Hymer's view of the multinational firm as an organization. His analysis implies that the retention of control over corporate strategy at the top level is an overriding principle. Top managers in multinational firms will evaluate all further geographic extension of the organization to guard against the possible negative impact such extension might have on their ability to retain absolute control.

## NOTES

1. In 1960 MIT refused to publish the thesis as a book as it was felt that it was not sufficiently analytical. When the virtues of the thesis were later realized as being the first attempt to explain foreign direct investment with a theory of the firm, it was eventually published in 1976.
2. Hymer also mentioned diversification as an independent factor motivating foreign direct investment. This factor, though, played a minor role in his analysis (Buckley 2006).

3. One example, originally described in John Dunning's early study of American investment in Britain (1958) deals with a market-sharing agreement between American Tobacco and the English Imperial Tobacco Company after a period of cut-throat competition, which included the formation of a joint venture between the two companies.

# 3. The Coordinating multinational: a tale of cost efficiency

## INTRODUCTION

In Chapter 2, I concluded that in Hymer's opinion foreign direct investment involved certain firms exploiting assets abroad that other firms did not possess. Based on industrial organization theory, he argued that monopolistic advantage was required for the phenomenon to occur. Without such an advantage, there would be no possibility of overcoming the liability of foreignness that a foreign investor inevitably experiences.

This simple fact became the main cornerstone for the subsequent development of the theory of the multinational firm during the 1970s and 1980s. Almost every scholar within the field accepted that market imperfection of some kind was a crucial platform from which a process of foreign direct investment can take off. In most cases, this market imperfection was expected to exist at a firm or industry level, rather than at the country level.[1]

Hymer and other scholars, though, had to explain why firms based in one country would be exploiting their advantage by undertaking production in another country. After all, production abroad means additional costs arising from the distance and a lack of market knowledge. Why not sell these assets through licensing to local entrepreneurs instead, who could then combine them with local factors of production at lower costs than those experienced by foreign investors (Hennart 1991)? An estimate of the amount of licensing as a proportion of all foreign direct investment in the mid 1970s showed that it was only about 10 per cent (Buckley and Davies 1979; see also Table 1.1 in Chapter 1). So, why was more licensing not conducted? Why did companies take the cumbersome route of entering into foreign investments on their own?

Hymer's answer to this was explicitly linked to his view on oligopolists' possibility of using their market power to attain higher profits, compared to operating in a situation of perfect competition, or at least less dominant market power, as would be the situation experienced by a local company operating under a licence. Thus, his explanation is explicitly about avoiding competition by incorporating two or more potential competitors under one and the same roof. The most obvious way of achieving this is by one firm acquiring another firm in the foreign market, or by arranging a merger between the two. Thus, two formerly independent agents are joined to form one multinational firm. In this way, it will be easier to keep price levels up and eliminate the losses they would inflict on each other through competition. Foreign direct investment will lead to a higher joint profit for the two agents, but not for society since the income is redistributed to the multinational firm, and not to the customers (Hennart 1991). The same reasoning can be also applied in the case of the multinational firm establishing an operation abroad from scratch, that is, without entering into a merger or acquisition, because this will eliminate potential competitors. Hymer's story, therefore, is one about using market power at the expense of others, and not only of exploiting a firm-specific asset in a more general sense.

This part of Hymer's analysis was much less accepted by his followers than the part concerning the necessity of an enterprise having a firm-specific advantage. As a matter of fact, during the 1970s and 1980s, the development of the theory of the multinational firm took another route, which will form the topic of this chapter.

There were several reasons for this new route. Firstly, some economists argued that perfect competition is an unrealistic and impractical policy benchmark. If multinational firms possess the upper hand, then perfect competition simply cannot prevail (Teece 2006). The conclusion would inevitably be that breaking up multinational firms is the only way to establish a higher degree of competition in the industry concerned – a policy that Hymer, to some extent, argued for. But the economists claimed that this simply does not reflect reality. Even if anti-trust policy is important, anti-trust economics tells us that there is a substantial gap between identifying a market imperfection and there being a monopoly problem that would warrant a public policy response. Or, as put forward by Teece: 'Even the competition authorities understand that monopoly power earned by proper conduct is desirable and there is quite some distance between finding monopoly and identifying behaviour that warrants legal or policy intervention and sanctions' (*op. cit.*, p. 127).

The difference between Hymer and some of his followers when it comes to the nature of exploitation of firm-specific advantages is an example of a more general conflict between radical and orthodox economists. Hymer's original intention was to explain why foreign direct investment occurs. In his later writing, though, he became increasingly inclined to question whether multinational firms always are the best solution to the allocation of resources and to income distribution in a society in which they operate. His concern was especially directed to the impact on economic development in developing economics. In that sense, his work is a reflection of the radicalization of politics, not least in relation to multinationals, during the 1960s and 1970s. This stands in sharp contrast to the work by most of the orthodox economists who focused on models intended to explain why multinational firms are contributing to the economic welfare of society. The work of the latter economists also coincides with a remarkable deradicalization of the debate about multinationals that took place during the 1980s and 1990s, compared to the discussion one or two decades earlier.

Secondly, Hymer's critics accused him of being very unspecific about the true nature of what a multinational firm's specific advantage is all about. Or, as one of the critics put it:

> Because there is no explanation of how the advantages are generated they appear in the (Hymer) theory as windfall gains, or 'manna from Heaven'. The planning and investment necessary to build up the advantages are ignored. This means that the theory overstates the average profitability of firms exploiting these advantages, because it ignores altogether their cost of acquisition. (Buckley and Casson 1991, p. 69)

Related to the issue of special advantage is the fact that researchers engaged in considering this problem became more and more inclined to link firm-specific advantage to concepts like knowledge and skills. In Chapter 2, I pointed out that some scholars argued that firm-specific advantages were basically intangible assets, developed over time inside the firm, and that they were difficult to separate from the firm itself. This advantage was neither the result of 'windfall gains', nor did it arrive like 'manna from Heaven'. It had certain properties that also needed certain measures to be taken if it were to be exploited. Hymer was inclined to consider firm-specific advantages as something that some firms have, but might not have earned. For him, the important thing is that they give them an (unfair) advantage over other firms. This is the core of his concern with market imperfection. In contrast, his followers perceived firm-specific advantage to be something that is inherently linked to the skill of an individual agent. It is earned by the firm and cannot be meaningfully shared with other firms. It is definitely a case of market imperfection, but rather than being a problem, is a fact of business life and associated with skill and knowledge as intangible assets.

These objections led some economists to adopt a different view on the basic drivers behind foreign direct investment. In comparison to Hymer, they devoted more attention to the multinational firm as an institution. While Hymer saw them as giant hierarchies that conquered the world through their strategy against real and potential competitors, based on market power, this new perspective paid more attention to what was actually going on inside the multinational firm. In the next section, the main thoughts behind this view, often called 'internalization theory', will be presented.

# INTERNALIZATION THEORY: A TALE OF COST EFFICIENCY

## The Issue of Coordination

The development of this new theory on the multinational firm, called 'internalization theory', starts with two basic, but related, premises. Firstly, business is about coordinating interdependent economic activities. A firm is one possible means of bringing about such coordination. Secondly, the characteristics of the firm-specific asset constitute an important explanation for why the multinational firm exists. The knowledge content of the asset, in particular, is crucial.

The first point deals with the fact that inside a typical firm, several activities are carried out. Many of these activities are related, in the sense that how one activity is carried out is dependent on how the activities before or after the focal activity are performed. A classic example is the activity chain in a company, comprised of purchasing, production and marketing. Within a step in such a chain, for instance production, there are also consecutive stages such as the processing of raw materials, the handling of intermediate products and finalizing the end product. All of these stages must be efficiently coordinated in one way or another. The fundamental questions put forward by proponents of internalization theory are: Why is this coordination apparently often carried out within one firm rather than between independent firms? Why are so many interdependent activities internalized? After all, coordination within the firm means administrative costs that could be avoided if the coordination could be carried out through the market system between independent actors.

The answer to the second question is associated the knowledge content of the asset that is being coordinated. Buckley and Casson, two well-known proponents of the internalization theory, summarize the reason for internalization in the following way: 'Firstly, the production of knowledge through R&D, and its implementation in new processes or products, are lengthy projects which require detailed long-term appraisal and careful short-term synchronization. In the absence of future markets, effective planning requires internalization of the market' (Buckley and Casson 1991, p. 39).

The following example illustrates the point. If a firm invests heavily in the production of a new product, it must have a certain level of confidence that the appropriate sales and marketing facilities will be to hand in the future when the product is to be commercialized. If the market cannot offer such a guarantee, there is a strong incentive for the firm to establish its own sales organization. This is the time aspect of internalization.

But there is also an uncertainty aspect. One reason for internalization is uncertainty about the value of a knowledge-intensive asset and the problem that this creates for the coordination of activities. To quote Buckley and Casson again:

> imperfection occurs when there is inequality between the buyer and seller with respect to knowledge of the nature or value of the product. If the seller of an intermediate product is better informed than the buyer, but for one reason or another is unable to convince the buyer that the price requested is reasonable, then the seller has an incentive to shoulder the buyer's risk, either by taking over the buyer, or setting up in competition with him. 'Buyer uncertainty' may therefore encourage forward integration. (Ibid., p. 38)

With reference to the example above, the more intangible the knowledge is upon which the new product is based, the more difficult it will be for a potential sales agent or distributor to assess the market potential of the new product. It will also be difficult for the seller to justify its value in such a way that the sales agent or distributor is prepared to invest in the new business. After all, the knowledge about the product is mainly locked up in the mind of the producer, and the more intangible the knowledge is, the more inaccessible it becomes. As a result of this, it will be difficult for the producer and the sales agent to agree upon investment to be made in marketing, the price of the product, commission rate, and so on. The negotiations between the producer and the potential sales agent run the risk of breaking down. Eventually, the producer decides to take care of sales and marketing himself, although this will mean a higher cost in terms of the investment in a sales force, administration, and so on. This is a typical case of internalizing through forward vertical integration and arises because the market has failed to meet the necessary transactions required between two steps in the value chain. The risk of such failure is obviously higher the more intangible the asset is upon which the product is based, because the uncertainty on the buyer side is especially high in such a situation.

**Why Multinationals?**

It is claimed by the proponents of internalization theory that the factors that drive the internalization of activities from markets into the firm are exactly the same factors that explain why there are multinational firms at all: the multinational firm exists because the firm has internalized markets across country borders. Owing to differences in location costs, some activities are more efficiently carried out in some countries than in others. If these activities need to be coordinated, and if the asset on which the need for coordination is based is of an intangible knowledge-intensive nature, the drive for internalization across borders is strong and a multinational firm is created.

This is the most general explanation of internalization theory for why we have multinational firms. In the example above, cost considerations may tell us that the production of a product under consideration is best in country A due to cheap labour, while the marketing of the product should be performed in country B because of the importance of the sales activities being close to end-customers. In such a case, there is sometimes an incentive to coordinate these activities inside the firm; that is, to create a multinational firm.

This incentive becomes stronger the more knowledge-intensive the product is.

Internalization theory does not totally exclude there being other reasons for foreign direct investments to be made than the factors above. For instance, Buckley and Casson point out that a bilateral monopoly can exist whereby the parties agree to avoid the market through some kind of joint arrangement. If, for instance, a firm has more or less exclusive rights to a product and wants to exploit the product in a foreign market, while another firm controls the distribution outlets and so on in that market, a potential bargaining conflict would be avoided by some form of vertical integration, through acquisition, a merger or a joint venture (Buckley and Casson 1991).

On the surface, this argument looks strikingly similar to Hymer's view of the removal of conflicts as a driver for foreign direct investment. But the resemblance is only skin-deep. To Hymer, the reason for joint ownership across borders was primarily that it offered a way to control competition and to benefit from above-normal prices. In the internalization theory, in contrast, the reason is to avoid an uncertain bargaining situation by moving the two counterparts under the same roof. In Hymer's view, the motivation is that of raising prices through foreign direct investment. In the latter theory, the issue is one of reducing costs by avoiding bargaining between independent actors. This is a crucial difference in perspective with far-reaching consequences for the way that the multinational firm is perceived from a social welfare point of view. But more about this later.

What about horizontal integration then? Horizontal integration means that units producing and marketing the same type of product or service are united under one firm. If these units are located in different countries, the firm is a multinational firm. What is the reason for such a solution? Why are the units in the different countries not operated as separate firms?

The explanation offered by internalization theory is quite similar to that for vertical integration, although in the horizontal case the coordination of activities is not the main issue. Again, the fact that firm-specific assets are often intangible provides the key. Suppose for a moment that, for some reason, a firm can produce a high-technology product in its home market that it also intends to exploit in a foreign market. Suppose, too, that for cost reasons it will be necessary to produce the products in the foreign market, because exporting them is not a realistic alternative, perhaps to high import tariffs. Selling a licence to a local company could be a tempting alternative as it could avoid making the investment of establishing its own production abroad and the administrative costs of controlling the foreign operations.

This strategy, though, would encounter several problems. Firstly, the transaction of the knowledge of how to produce the product from the holder of this knowledge to a potential licensee in the foreign market may be costly. This problem is best explained by an example from another spokesman of internalization theory:

> I have a piece of knowledge that I know will be valuable to you. I try to convince you of this value by describing its general nature and character. But I do not reveal the details, because then the cat would be out of the bag, and you would be free to use the knowledge without paying for it (unless, of course, I have established a property right in the technology that allows me to exclude those users who have not paid my asking price. Patents, copyrights, and trademarks are just such property rights). But you therefore decline to pay me as much as the knowledge would in fact be worth to you, because you suspect that I am opportunistic and overstate my claims. With these conditions present, I cannot collect the full net-revenue productivity of my knowledge. I will under-invest in the knowledge, or maybe try to earn the most I can from that knowledge I do acquire by putting it to work myself. (Caves 1982, p. 5)

This is a typical example of opportunism, which makes transactions in a market costly. Opportunism is especially prevalent when it is hard to separate the knowledge from the holder of the knowledge because it carries a high proportion of intangible know-how. It is argued that internalization in terms of a foreign direct investment will solve this problem.

Secondly, uncertainty can amplify the problem of high transaction costs. Another quote from Caves illustrates this problem:

> If the knowledge were a recipe for a truly superb chocolate cake, I could bring about an efficient arm's-length transaction by letting you taste the cake and guaranteeing that (once you have bought the recipe and executed it properly) yours will taste just as good. Conversely, if neither of us can predict accurately how well the knowledge will perform when you use it, and if we are both risk-averse, too small a volume of transactions will take place in the intangible knowledge. (*Op. cit.*, p. 5)

Uncertainty, therefore, also leads to a strategy of avoiding the market (in terms of licensing, and so on) through pursuit of one's own exploitation (that is, to engage in foreign direct investment). This strategy will lead to a reduction of transaction costs compared to the market solution.

We can conclude that the basic reasons for internalization are very similar in the cases of vertical and horizontal integration. In both cases, information asymmetry between potential transaction partners, opportunism, uncertainty and the problem of separating the knowledge from the firm that possesses it, are the basic reasons for market failure. These problems are more serious the more intangible the knowledge is. In the case of vertical integration, though, the need for coordination implies a special concern related to future deliveries of products and services from interdependent activities

**Transaction Cost Economics**

The view that the firm is an organization internalizing markets across borders has much in common with transaction cost economics (TCE) (Buckley and Casson 1991; Cantwell 1991). There are essentially four components in TCE: uncertainty, small-numbers bargaining, bounded rationality and opportunism (Williamson, 1975).

Uncertainty refers to the changes in the environment that the owner of a firm-specific asset cannot foresee or control. It provides a dynamic element that makes the existence of a market unstable. Small-numbers bargaining means that once a long-term contract has been signed with suppliers, employees or customers, the normal market situation is disturbed. The parties to the contract have privileged positions, which make changing partners difficult. If, for instance, a firm invests in its relationship with a certain supplier, in terms of gaining experience of working with the supplier, establishing routines, and so on, it becomes difficult to substitute this supplier with another one if the present supplier's quality slips. A related concept is 'asset specificity'. Market transactions often involve transaction-specific investments due to adaptation of resources to a specific counterpart. The higher the asset specificity, the more difficult it is to find an alternative usage for these resources, which gives the counterpart some bargaining power.

Bounded rationality reflects imperfect information about suppliers and customers in the market. This, in turn, creates problems because of opportunism. For instance, a supplier claims that owing to problems related to raw materials, it will not be able to deliver on time. The buyer has no way to assess whether this is true or not, but since another supplier cannot suddenly meet the corresponding need, and since it is expensive to guard against such problems, the buyer is at the mercy of the supplier (Perrow 1986).

TCE tells us that the four components all contribute to high transaction costs in the market. To some extent the problem can be dealt with by collecting more information about transaction partners, through bargaining more between partners, by specifying contracts, and so on. But all of these efforts are costly. TCE predicts, though, that when these costs attain a certain level, the market will be substituted by the hierarchy in terms of a firm. The reason for this is that the hierarchy is better equipped to take care of the costs related to all four components. For instance, opportunism is curbed when the transaction takes place between two subunits in one and the same firm because the transaction is controlled by the firm's management. Bounded rationality is not believed to be a problem for the management inside the firm, just between counterparts in the market. Therefore, the subunits have no reason for or possibility of cheating, they just obey orders. Similarly, inside the firm, small-numbers bargaining and asset specificity are not problems in themselves, but rather they are natural parts of the firm's coordination of activities.

The basic conclusion of TCE, therefore, is that the scale of the firm is set at the margin where the benefits and costs of further internalization are equalized (Buckley and Casson 1991). The benefits of internalization are the reduction in the cost of transactions compared to the market solution. The costs of internalization are the increased administrative costs required to control the transaction inside the firm compared to the market solution. In principle, all firms have an optimal size, otherwise the firm could save money by increasing or decreasing its scale of operation.

Internalization theory means that the same reasoning is employed in the multinational firm. Every multinational has a certain size, because at that size the sum of its transaction costs (in the market) and its administrative costs (inside the firm) is minimized. The simple reason for calling the firm a multinational firm is that some of the activities that are internalized are carried out in different countries. In that sense, the internalization theory is less a specific theory on multinational firms, and more a theory about firms in general, whether national or international.

Recently the concept of the global factory has been introduced as a special application of internalization theory (Buckley 2010). The global factories:

> choose location and ownership policies as to maximize profits but this does not necessarily involve internalizing their activities. Indeed they have set a trend by outsourcing or offshoring their activities . . . MNEs have developed the ability to 'fine slice' their activities on an even more precise calculus and are increasingly able to alter location and internalization decisions for activities which were previously locationally bound by being tied to other activities and which could only be controlled by internal management fiat. (*Op. cit.*, p. 60)

The concept of the global factory implies that geographic location and whether to make or buy are explicit strategic decisions, and in that sense becomes more a specific theory on multinational firms rather than a theory on firms in general. However, the reasoning is nevertheless founded on the basic assumption of internalization theory that the size of the firm, as a legal entity, reflects the level of transaction costs and administrative costs.

## INTERNALIZATION THEORY AND THE SOCIETAL ROLE OF THE MULTINATIONAL FIRM

Hymer's perspective on multinational firms implies a critical analysis of the multinational firm as a phenomenon. During the 1960s and 1970s, the criticism of the multinationals was also quite common. During the 1980s and 1990s, though, the majority of scholars fell silent on this issue. One reason for this change was probably the introduction of internalization theory. Although it has been claimed that Hymer was very well aware of the transaction cost problem (Horaguichi and Toyne 1990), it is nevertheless true that his concern was related to supposed above-normal profits and monopolistic behaviour.[2] Internalization theory tells us a different story. The establishment and growth of the multinational firm is essentially interpreted as cost-minimizing behaviour rather than as rent-seeking monopolistic behaviour. The multinational firm ends where the sum of transaction costs and administrative costs is minimized.

This difference also leads to different conclusions concerning the socio-political role of the multinational firm. Both theories deal with market imperfections, but the views taken on market imperfections differ quite considerably. Hymer emphasized differences between firms in terms of the competitive situation, reflected in concepts like market structure, barriers to entry and so on. The imperfections he considered are, thus, primarily structural (Hennart 1982). Internalization theory deals with market imperfection in terms of inadequacies in market pricing arising from uncertainty, small-numbers bargaining, bounded rationality and opportunism. These imperfections are inherent parts of the products or services in question – and of human nature – and there is very little one can do about them. Thus, these imperfections are natural rather than structural (Hennart *op. cit.*).

Structural imperfections can lead to above-normal profits for the multinational firms, but losses for the society in which the company operates. The impact of natural imperfections is of a different kind. The multinational firm maximizes its profits by minimizing its costs (that is, its transaction costs and administrative costs). This will lead to a net gain, not only for the firm, but also for the society. Market power is substituted by cost efficiency, and there is no reason to question the success of internalization as a means of avoiding market failure. Consequently, the growth and the size of the multinational firms are not important political issues in the internalization theory. We have the firms we deserve. Even in the extreme case of an industry consisting only of one firm, there is in principle no room in internalization theory to question its efficiency. Every situation is dictated by avoiding natural imperfections through the hierarchy. The reason why the number of firms differs between industries, then, is that all markets do not suffer from high transaction costs to the same extent.

This view results in quite effective disarming of most attempts to question the multinational firm. Internalization theory dominated the research field during the 1980s and 1990s, which is probably one important explanation for the decline in the critical analysis of the multinational firm throughout these two decades. The theory just did not offer the right tools for such an analysis.

However, a closer look reveals that even if there are fundamental differences between the two perspectives, they are not mutually exclusive. Above all, internalization theory considers market

44        *Theories of the multinational firm*

imperfections to be the main stimulus for the establishment of multinational firms through foreign direct investments. Although this is also an important part of Hymer's model, his main focus increasingly came to be the behaviour of the multinational firms once they had been created. Internalization can be relevant as an explanation for foreign direct investments, but that does not exclude the possibility that multinational firms are in an especially favourable position to reduce competition in the market through horizontal mergers, strategic alliances, bargaining with governments and so on, with possible negative consequences for society. That is, exploitation of market power is not entirely an alien concept in internalization theory. However, if transaction cost economists find little reason to question the establishment of the multinational firm, they also probably find it less relevant to criticize its conduct after the firm has become multinational.

The difference between the market power argument and the cost-efficiency argument is apparent when it comes to the growth of the firm. In internalization theory, the issue is savings on transaction costs. Firms grow because they internalize activities either horizontally or vertically. In Hymer's opinion internalization is primarily a consequence of an ambition to control the market. Or, as expressed by Perrow:

> The major industries of the United States – oil and chemicals, iron, steel, automobiles, electrical goods, food processing, railroads, and now electronics and television – are as concentrated as they are not because the leading firms saved on transactions costs or were efficient in other ways, but because they could control the market, labor, and government and were backed up by powerful financial interests. (Perrow 1986, p. 247)

One may express the linkage between the transaction cost argument and the market power argument in the following way: the firm's growth in response to its effort in economizing on transaction costs leads to a larger and more powerful firm, and thus probably to more structural imperfections. A larger firm can access and process higher levels of information and it operates with high levels of asset specificity. These elements will increase its tendency towards internalization and thus towards more structural imperfections in a vicious circle (Ietto-Gillies 2012).

# WHAT DOES THE MULTINATIONAL FIRM LOOK LIKE IN INTERNALIZATION THEORY?

## The Principle of Behaviour Constraints

The basic idea behind TCE is that the market and the firm offer alternative ways to organize economic activities. Therefore, it is extremely important that there is a fundamental difference between the market and the firm, as an organization. A step from the market into the firm corresponds to a radical change in the ability to control the activity in question. Thus, TCE implies that multinationals ought to be pure hierarchies in which the bosses have (or ought to have) complete control over what their subordinates are doing and the competence they possess.

Consequently, control is an extremely important issue in internalization theory. Through information from below and control from above, transaction costs attributable to bounded rationality and opportunism are supposed to be eliminated or, at least, be minimized. If the firm does not manage to control the transactions in that sense, the whole idea behind increased cost efficiency through internalization collapses. As bounded rationality and opportunism are such crucial issues, the matter of control in TCE relies on 'behaviour constraints'. Or as expressed by one of the advocates of TCE:

> the essence of firms is the employment relationship (i.e. the imposition of behavior constraints). It is by imposing behavior constraints (and simultaneously relaxing price constraints) that the cost . . . is reduced. Hence the use of hierarchy (behavior constraints) is the distinguishing mark of firms. The use of employment contracts, in which the employee is rewarded entirely in relation to his or her obedience to managerial directives, is widespread in firms. (Hennart 1993, p. 165)

Thus, constraining behaviour through the issuing of orders from higher up the chain of command to those below is the overriding principle of organization in a firm. Replacing the price system in a market with contracts between the firm and its employees implies a separation between the employees' output and the employees' rewards. Therefore, employees have no reason to try to increase their (short-term) output by cheating in their transactions with other subunits – which was a problem in market transactions – because such behaviour will not affect their rewards. Reward is entirely linked to obedience to orders. Hence, transaction costs related to opportunism disappear inside the firm.

## The Problem of Information Asymmetry and Shirking

One problem, though, pops up when activities are internalized. In order to be able to voice or draft clear directives to guide employees' behaviour, management needs to know what the employee must do to generate the desired output. That is, the bosses need to comprehend the employee's production function (Hennart 1993). But where many individuals are concerned this becomes an overwhelming task for the management, not least in large multinational firms. Therefore, the firm suffers from the classical information asymmetry problem: management does not possess the required information on the activities at lower levels, as a result of which it is also difficult to give appropriate orders. This will decrease the administrative efficiency of the organization.

Another problem is shirking. In TCE, the market is supposed to be efficient if the price mechanism functions properly. The actors in the market do their best, and if they decide to shirk, the first result will be a decline in their own output and, therefore, their own reward. Inside the firm, though, as the reward is separated from the output through a contract with the employer, shirking is a bigger problem. This, at least, is how it is perceived from a TCE perspective.

The classical solution in TCE theory to both information asymmetry and shirking is decentralization. By substituting direct control through order-giving with output control – that is, controlling the output rather than the process that leads to a certain output – the need for information processing at the headquarters is reduced. For instance, in a multinational firm, subsidiaries can be treated as independent profit centres. By choosing appropriate internal transfer prices, the firm can elicit the same behaviour as it would through direct behaviour control. If output is measurable, and headquarters has less knowledge than the subsidiary manager about how to achieve the desired outcome, then leaving subsidiary managers free to maximize the subsidiary's profits (and rewarding them as a function of these profits) will achieve better results than specifically directing their behaviour through directives from headquarters (Hennart 1993).

Treating subsidiaries as profit centres and rewarding them as a function of their profits also implies that the problem of shirking inside the firm decreases. The link between output and reward, which is such an important characteristic of an efficient market, is restored. Or, expressed differently, the market is mirrored inside the firm. So, if there is no problem with shirking in the market, profit-centre control will lead to at least reduced shirking inside the firm. In the extreme case of profit-centre control, that is, when the sub-units are free to set the transfer prices through a bargaining process (including freedom to buy from or sell to independent firms), there will be no problem of shirking.

**Curb the Cheating or Curb the Shirking?**

This reasoning, though, discloses an inherent dilemma in the way that TCE and internalization theory deal with the issue of control. On one hand, the perspective assumes that opportunistic behaviour through cheating in the market is an important reason why firms internalize activities (and why firms become multinational). Consequently, curbing such behaviour through the hierarchy is crucial. Advocates of this perspective state that such behaviour is controlled by clearly separating reward (in the form of the employees' pay) from output, because in such a situation there is no reason for opportunistic behaviour. This is actually supposed to be 'the distinguishing mark of firms' (Hennart 1993, p. 165).

On the other hand, if shirking inside the firm is also a serious problem – which it usually is in this perspective – and the solution to shirking is to create some kind of market inside the firm by restoring the link between reward and output, some degree of suboptimization inevitably exists. If shirking is reduced through the specific design of the control system, the firm runs the risk of losing its ability to curb cheating behaviour, which was the intention of the internalization in the first place. On the contrary, if the firm applies behaviour control, rather than output control, the problem of shirking is apparent. In principle, the firm cannot solve problems associated with cheating and shirking at the same time.

A common line of reasoning in the TCE literature is that behaviour control through centralization is applied when the firm experiences a high level of cheating but little shirking, while profit-centre control is used when shirking is more problematic than cheating (Hennart

1993). But there is no reason to expect that the two problems are inversely related. On the contrary, from a TCE perspective, it is reasonable to argue that cheating and shirking exist to more or less the same degree as they are both firmly rooted in human nature. TCE does not seem to have any solution to the control problem when there is a high level of cheating and of shirking. This is serious as the TCE perspective emphasizes that cheating and shirking are the most crucial issues in terms of control.

**The Issue of Control in Internalization Theory**

The reasoning above indicates that TCE applies a very instrumental view to the firm as an organization. The firm is seen primarily as a hierarchy, although with different degrees of decentralization of decision-making. In internalization theory, this is reflected in the way the issue of the control of subsidiaries is treated. Firstly, control is basically about the vertical relationship between the headquarters and its subsidiaries. Lateral relationships between subsidiaries do not fall within the control issue. Secondly, the basic question is how the headquarters are to get the subsidiaries to do what they want them to do. The answer is all about monitoring the subsidiaries, one by one, essentially leaving no room for initiatives from below. Thirdly, although it is recognized that certain knowledge can reside more or less at the subsidiary level, rather than at the headquarters level, leading to information asymmetry, there is no doubt that the power resides at the top of the hierarchy. This implies that the headquarters solely designs the organization in a way that ensures that optimal control over the subsidiaries is attained. Fourthly, the multinational firm is primarily an instrument for carrying out the intentions of the headquarters, rather than of the subsidiaries. Fifthly, subsidiaries are generally perceived as problem generators, in the sense that if they are not monitored properly, their behaviour will be dominated by their inherent lust to cheat and shirk.

The last point is illustrated by the quotation below from one of the advocates of TCE, reflecting how it perceives human behaviour:

> Unfortunately, unless all dimensions of performance are measured and priced (or constrained), maximization of effort may lead to maximization of unwanted side-effects: for example, paying piece rates for picking crabs (for extracting their meat) will incite workers to extract only the

easy-to-remove back meat and to leave claw-meat in the shells. This tendency is easily checked by weighing the picked shells and deducting from the picker's earnings a penalty proportional to the weight of the shells. This discourages pickers from leaving too much meat in shells. (Hennart 1993, p. 169)

Monitoring is the word!

To sum up, like the attitude adopted by Hymer, TCE and internalization theory perceive the multinational firm to be a pure hierarchy. The headquarters has complete power over the activities of its employees and designs the organization in accordance with its goals. But while Hymer, at least implicitly, saw this as a problem, internalization theory sees it as a necessity. Hymer was concerned by the high concentration of power in the upper echelons of the giant multinational firms, and claimed that this distortion of power created an imbalance in terms of income and economic development between countries. There is limited room for such concern in internalization theory. On the contrary, as the theory is obsessed with the headquarters' monitoring of the subunits, power concentration at the top is a must. The main focus is on how this monitoring should be carried out so that the advantage of a hierarchy over a market can be reaped to the full.

## THE ECLECTIC FRAMEWORK

Hymer's view offers an explanation to the question of why foreign investments are possible in the first place: some firms possess advantages that others do not. Internalization theory deals mainly with the 'how' issue: in which situations do firm choose to internalize their foreign operations? Neither of these theories, though, addresses the question of where the firm chooses to place its foreign activities. After all, countries differ when it comes to distance, culture, institutions, trade barriers, and so on. From Hymer's perspective, countries play a role insofar as business conditions differ between the home country and other countries. Thus the firm's lack of knowledge about foreign countries is an important part of the model. But why the firm is located in a certain country rather than in any other country is not treated in any detail. In internalization theory, the country plays an even less significant role, although the reasoning starts by assuming that, for efficiency reasons, different parts of the operation must be located in different countries. But the choice to internalize has little to do with country borders. It is a theory more concerned with internalization than internationalization (Ietto-Gillies 2012).

The lack of importance assigned to location in these theories made John Dunning suggest that a fully fledged theory of foreign direct investment must not only include firm-specific advantages and advantages arising from internalization, but also location-specific advantages (Dunning 1988, 1997). The latter, as the name implies, are all linked to the geographic and political space and, as such, include the cost and quality of transportation, the legal and commercial infrastructure, government policies, local access to raw material, and technology and human capital. These factors are as important as the firm's own advantages and its tendency to internalize its operations in shaping the firm's internationalization. Dunning's point is that although location-specific advantages are dependent on specific locations, they arise from a combination of firm-specific advantages and locally based resources and capabilities. For instance, an oil company must invest in oil extraction where the oil is located, but the investment is dependent on the firm's own technology, and on how well it can build up and run such an operation. This investment also implies that internalization is more cost efficient than externalization.

Therefore, it is the interplay between firm-specific advantage (which Dunning chooses to call 'ownership advantage', to emphasize the fact that this is an advantage controlled by the individual firm), internalization advantage and location-specific advantage that makes up what Dunning calls the 'eclectic framework'. Sometimes the location-specific advantages can be rather dominant in this interplay; for instance, if a country implements a policy offering strong subsidies to foreign investors – Ireland is a good example – this policy will have a strong impact on firms' investment behaviour.

Location-specific advantage in business activities has been an important issue in economics since more than a century ago (see for example Marshall 1890). Over the last decade, the concept of the cluster, indicating that firms tend to agglomerate in certain geographical spaces, has grown in importance. Although the exact meaning of a cluster varies between different authors, for our purpose it is sufficient to define a cluster as a geographic agglomeration of firms with similar and/or complementary business (Richardson 1972; Maskell and Malmberg 2007). Usual examples of clusters are Silicon Valley in the USA, Baden-Wurttenberg in Germany and Cambridge in Great Britain. The basic theme behind the cluster concept is that firms that have similar needs in terms of resources and capabilities have easier access to these resources if they are geographically close to each other. It is a dynamic concept in the sense that firms with similar needs and located in a specific place will attract resources that fulfil these needs, for example human resources or certain technologies. The concentration of such resources will further attract other firms to locate in such an area, and so on.

An important idea related to the cluster concept is that firms that belong to the same cluster benefit from different types of information spillover within the cluster. For example, a reason for a firm to locate in Silicon Valley might be an expectation that such a location will improve its possibilities of picking up information about the next step in the development in computer technology. Or phrased differently, it is assumed that barriers to information and, therefore, information transfer costs are lower between firms within a cluster than between other firms. This idea is strikingly similar to the TCE logic: an economic activity is organized so that it will minimize information transaction costs. The crucial difference, though, between the TCE applied to the multinational firm and the cluster concept is that in the former case the multinational firm is created in order internalize information transaction costs within a firm (a hierarchy), while clustering is a way to internalize information transaction costs between firms (McCann and Mudambi 2005). This difference points at the inherent conflict between the location-specific advantage and the internalization-specific advantage in the eclectic framework, at least if we emphasize the cluster aspect related to the former concept. Internalization advantage is defined as an advantage that depends on relationships between units within the same hierarchy, while location-specific advantage in a cluster depends on relationships with other firms. If a multinational firm chooses to locate a subsidiary in a specific cluster (in order to benefit from location-specific advantage), it might lead to a limited possibility of integrating the subsidiary in the multinational firm's intra-organizational information flow (in order to benefit from internalization advantage), due for example to the geographical or cultural distances between the parent company and the subsidiary. Correspondingly, if the multinational firm optimizes its internalization advantage through minimizing its internal information transaction costs, this might be detrimental to its possibility of reaching location-specific advantage through participating in different clusters.

Obviously, there are ample evidences of a trade-off between internalization advantage and location-specific advantage through clustering. Consequently, the combination of these two types of advantages is much more complicated than is usually suggested by the eclectic framework. Rather than complementing or reinforcing each other they tend to be competing factors in the geographical configuration of the multinational firm. The fundamental reason behind this conclusion is that internalization advantage deals with how to benefit from the fact that the firm is a hierarchy, leaving the relationship with the environment aside; while location-specific advantage is quite the opposite: how to benefit from relationships with other economic actors in specific locations, leaving the intra-organizational problems aside. This conclusion points to the fact that there is always an inbuilt tension between intra-organizational relationships and interorganizational relationships that every multinational firm has to deal with. This tension is a main theme in the conceptualization of the multinational firm as a Networking multinational. I will return to this issue in Chapter 6.

Lately the interplay between ownership advantage and location-specific advantage has had a more dynamic interpretation. It reflects the fact that many multinationals today are seen as geographically dispersed networks rather than firms that exploit a firm-specific advantage, developed in the home country, in a particular host country (Cantwell and Piscitello 2000). Even though the initial ownership advantage made the first steps in the internationalization possible, the further development of this advantage is linked to the fact that the firm operates in different business environments. That is, the network is in itself a competence-creating force. The ability to consolidate and extend the ownership advantage is very much dependent on the network of competence-creating subsidiaries (Cantwell and Narula 2001). The location advantage, therefore, is in fact not an exogenous but an endogenously created advantage (Cantwell 1989). It has been argued that the multinational firm has become more and more sophisticated in geographically slicing the firm's activities in combination with more complex ownership strategies (Buckley and Ghauri 2004).

Finally, it should be pointed out that the inclusion of location-specific advantages does not change the basic underpinning of internalization theory when it comes to perceiving the multinational firm as an organization or when considering its societal role. The overriding issue is still cost efficiency rather than market power.

## SUMMARY

Hymer's original intention was to answer the question: How is it that a national firm can start an operation in a foreign country? Internalization theory tries to answer a somewhat different question: Why is this operation carried out by the firm itself, and not sold to a local firm through the issue of, for instance, a licence?

The answer to the latter question requires an elaboration of what a firm is all about and why it is natural to internalize activities within a firm. In internalization theory, the firm is primarily an alternative to the market as a place in which to coordinate economic activities. It is argued that sometimes, and mainly because of the knowledge content of the products in question, the market fails to carry out such coordination in an efficient way.

The main reason for the market failure is the existence of uncertainty, small-numbers bargaining, bounded rationality and opportunistic behaviour. Uncertainty has to do with the changes in the environment that the owner of a monopolistic advantage cannot foresee or control. Small-numbers bargaining means that the counterparts in a business transaction find themselves locked into the relationship, and the more so, the more they have adapted their resources and operations to each other; that is, the higher their asset specificity. Bounded rationality reflects imperfect information about suppliers and customers in the market. Finally, opportunistic behaviour means that counterparts have a possibility and a tendency to cheat because of bounded rationality.

One main conclusion in transaction cost economics (TCE), on which internalization theory is based, is that these four components lead to high transaction costs in the market. Another main conclusion is that these costs can be eliminated, or at least substantially reduced, if the coordination is carried out within one and the same firm. That is, if the operations are internalized. Consequently, a firm is created because up to some level, it is more efficient to coordinate activities inside a firm than to carry them out through transactions between independent firms in a market. Or, expressed in a different way, the scale of the firm is set at the margin where the benefits from and costs of further internalization are equalized.

In line with TCE, internalization theory claims that the multinational firm exists because the firm has internalized markets across country borders. Therefore, the establishment of the multinational firm is interpreted as a form of cost-minimizing behaviour. The border of the multinational firm ends where the sum of transaction costs (in the external market) and administrative costs (inside the firm) is minimized. This stands in sharp contrast to Hymer's opinion that the existence of the multinational firm is closely linked to rent-seeking, monopolistic behaviour.

This difference is crucial for the socio-political role of the multinational firm. Hymer emphasized differences between firms in terms of competition, reflected in concepts like market structure and barriers to entry. These imperfections are mainly structural. In contrast, internalization theory deals with market imperfections in terms of inadequacies in market pricing arising from uncertainty, small-numbers bargaining, bounded rationality and opportunism. These imperfections are rooted in the product or service in question – and in human nature – and, therefore, are impossible to change. The imperfections are natural, rather than structural. While structural imperfections can lead to above-normal profits and losses for the society in which the company is based, if the multinational firm exists because of internalizing caused by natural market imperfections, this is also a net gain for society. Or, expressed differently, there is no room for a critical analysis of the socio-political role of the multinational firm in internalization theory.

Because of the importance of drawing a sharp demarcation between the market and the firm, the model of the firm as an organization is quite distinct in internalization theory. The theory adopts an extremely hierarchical and instrumental view. The exertion of control over the subunits by the headquarters through behaviour constraints is the overriding principle, through which cheating and shirking will be kept in check. All power is concentrated at headquarters, which designs the organization in accordance with its goals.

John Dunning has suggested that a fully fledged theory of foreign direct investment should also include a geographic dimension, because multinational firms do not only benefit from firm-specific and internalization advantages, but also from what he called 'location-specific advantage'. It is the interplay between these three different types of advantages that makes up what he calls the 'eclectic framework'. It was pointed out, though, that to the extent location-specific advantage is reflected in firms' agglomeration in clusters, a conflict between internalization advantage and location-specific advantage might appear. The reason is that the former advantage builds on the fact that the hierarchy is used to optimize intra-organizational relationships, while the latter advantage is reached by optimizing the relationships with other firms in the cluster.

## NOTES

1. There are exceptions, though. The most well-known example is Aliber's suggestion that foreign direct investments reflect the fact that firms from hard-currency countries can raise capital in host countries more cheaply than local firms. This explanation must be judged against the dominance of US investments abroad at the time when the idea was launched. Although it can be claimed that this is also an example of a monopolistic advantage, it is an advantage at the country level, which fails to explain cross-border investments (Aliber 1970).

2. That Hymer was aware of the transaction cost aspect already in his thesis is reflected in an often cited passage in his thesis: 'the firm internalizes or supercedes the market – decentralized decision-making (i.e. a free market) is defective when there are certain types of interactions between firms; that is each firm's behaviour noticeably affects the other firms' (Hymer 1976, p. 48). This aspect, though, did not influence his model of the multinational firm in a more profound way.

# 4. The Knowing multinational: a tale of value creation

## INTRODUCTION

The reasoning in Chapter 2 leads to the conclusion that there would be no stimulus for foreign direct investments to be made in the presence of perfect competition. For a firm to establish an operation in a foreign country, it must possess a specific advantage that is strong enough to counterbalance the disadvantage arising from the liability of being foreign. This firm-specific advantage constitutes the market power on which the firm bases its internationalization. The internationalization will further strengthen the firm's market power through collusion within oligopolies in the global market place. The market power model relies on the diffusion of knowledge from the parent company in the home country to affiliates in other countries. It is also concerned with competition and market position. The firm-specific advantage is essentially an advantage over other firms, and particularly over the firms in the potential host countries, which give the foreign investor the ability to enter the new market. One manifestation of such an advantage is a differentiated product, which creates a surplus in the market.

In Chapter 3, a different picture evolves. Although firm-specific advantage is recognized as an important element in internalization theory, it is the 'internalization advantage' that is brought to the fore. Firms are created because they can handle transactions of assets more efficiently than the market. In this way, the cost associated with uncertainty, small-numbers bargaining, bounded rationality and opportunism can be avoided or reduced more easily inside the firm than between independent firms. This is especially important when the knowledge associated with the asset is tacit. The reason for this internalization advantage is closely linked to the attribute of the hierarchy as a monitoring system. Through the hierarchy, the transactions can be controlled in such a way that transaction costs are eliminated. When the internalization includes several countries, a multinational firm is established.

In Hymer's approach, the driver for the firm going abroad and becoming a multinational is its ability to exploit monopoly rents. In the internalization approach, it is the firm's ability to reach a higher degree of cost efficiency. Firms become multinational because they are more cost efficient than the market. So, in contrast to the argument concerning market power, it is not the monopolistic advantage per se that makes the difference. It is the firm as an institution, a hierarchy. In addition internalization is not primarily about diffusion of knowledge from one country to others, but rather, it is about coordinating interdependent activities that, for economic reasons, are located in different countries.

As mentioned in Chapter 3, advocates of the internalization theory claimed that Hymer's model was unspecific about the true nature of the firm-specific advantage. It was like 'windfall gains' or 'manna from heaven'. It is reasonable to argue, though, that this also goes for internalization theory itself. Although the theory claims that the nature of the asset on which the firm-specific advantage is based has an impact on the benefits of internalization, the true nature of the asset is analysed only to the extent that it has an impact on uncertainty, bounded rationality and opportunism. But how the asset has been built up and why it is firm-specific is not a main issue in internalization theory. For instance, if one firm has the ability to produce a certain product more efficiently than others, why can other firms not just imitate the technology? Why is the ability linked to a certain firm? Why is the advantage firm-specific?

The main issue in internalization theory is that the firm creates an advantage through internalizing a market transaction. But as the theory assumes that this is what firms do up to the point where the sum of transaction cost and control cost is minimized, the internalization advantage is far from firm-specific. On the contrary, it is an 'advantage' that all firms have, whether domestic or multinational, owing to their ability to use their hierarchies for efficient control.

During the 1990s some researchers started to develop the concept of firm-specific advantage as intended by Hymer and as incorporated in internalization theory. In relation to the latter theory especially, some researchers felt uncomfortable with the underlying assumption that, at least in principle, the firm-specific asset could be traded. The justification for internalization is the relatively favourable transaction of an asset between subunits within a firm in comparison to a transaction involving the same asset in the market. In that sense, trading the asset in question is always an alternative, although this will sometimes involve high transaction costs. But what if trading the asset is not possible in the first place? Suppose that the asset is of such a nature that it is impossible to separate it from the firm that holds it. How could it be traded then? Maybe the asset is ingrained in the 'walls' of the firm, in the systems, people and routines. If that is the case, the asset cannot be moved to another firm without a severe reduction in its value.

Consequently, how relevant is it to talk about transaction costs, when entering into a transaction is not a realistic alternative? Or expressed differently, the exploitation of a firm-specific advantage can be reduced to a more basic issue, concerning the feasibility of transferring an asset rather than of overcoming the transaction costs.

The issue of feasibility is especially important for transfer within multinational firms, as the strategy of these firms is to exploit an asset in more than one country. The ability to transfer an asset from the home country to more distant markets often implies not only moving a certain piece of clearly defined knowledge from one geographic place to another, but also moving necessary routines and competences stored in individuals' minds. The decision on how that should be done does not depend on the costs arising from negotiations with a potential receiver associated with uncertainty and opportunism. Rather, the issue is how this can be done without losing too much value owing to the difficulty of establishing the necessary routines and competences in the new place. The more distant the new markets are, the more difficult that might be, not least in the context of the multinational firm. Therefore, it is important to explore the true nature of what Hymer and internalization theory called firm-specific advantage.

During the 1990s several scholars analysed the essence of firm-specific advantage under different labels, such as the resource-based view, the organization capability view, the dynamic capability view and the evolutionary theory of the multinational firm. Although the perspectives adopted emphasize different aspects of firm-specific advantage, they exhibit some common characteristics. Firstly, in contrast to earlier theories, they try to link the advantage more explicitly to the individual firm. It is the uniqueness of a firm that is the subject of consideration. Secondly, the existence of a symbiotic relationship between creation and exploitation of an asset is stressed. It is impossible to understand the conditions for exploiting an asset without considering the creation of that asset. Thus, the value of an asset is path-dependent, which makes it difficult to separate its exploitation from the institutional settings in which it was created (Cantwell and Piscitello 2000). Thirdly, a more sociological perspective of firms is applied. Perceiving the firm as a 'repository of knowledge' indicates that this knowledge is stored as much in the minds of people as in physical facilities. The firm is sometimes conceptualized as a 'social community' with a common identity amongst individuals rather than as a technical instrument, as was the case in internalization theory (Kogut and Zander 2003). Fourthly, the firm-specific knowledge can be dispersed throughout the organization. In the setting of a multinational firm, this implies that not only the parent company, but also the subsidiaries are in possession of knowledge contributing to the firm's competitive advantage. Fifthly, the crucial knowledge is primarily a capability. Thus, it comes down to 'know how' as much as 'know what'. This also has an impact on the possibility of transferring the asset to another setting, for instance, another country. Sixthly, the behaviour of a firm must also be understood in the light of the need to create, preserve and extend the competitive advantage. This implies that foreign direct investment and the operations of multinational firms reflect attempts to develop new capabilities as well as reflecting the exploitation of capabilities. Value creation is a key term in all of the different perspectives.

One of these perspectives is especially relevant for theorizing about foreign direct investment and the multinational firm, namely, the organizational capability perspective, including the evolutionary theory of the multinational firm. In the following I take a closer look at this perspective.

## ORGANIZATIONAL CAPABILITY VIEW AND THE MULTINATIONAL FIRM

As far as Hymer was concerned, firm-specific advantage is manifested primarily in the firm's final product and its market position vis-à-vis its competitors. In internalization theory the firm-specific advantage is mainly manifested in the firm's ability to reduce transaction costs through efficient monitoring of the production process.

In the 'organization capability' (OC) view, the firm-specific advantage is considered to encompass a great deal more than just the ability to reduce transaction costs. It reflects the uniqueness of each firm, including its history, people and organization. The advantage of the firm lies primarily within its managerial and organizational processes, and is shaped by its specific 'asset position' and the 'path' available to it. Managerial and organizational processes refer to the way things are done in the firm, or what might be called its routines and the patterns of its current practices. The 'asset position' is the firm's current specific endowments in terms of technology included in its intellectual property, complementary assets, customer base and its external relations with suppliers. By 'path', OC is referring to the strategic alternatives available to the firm, which are likely to be modelled on what it has done in the past (Teece et al. 1997). Behind this conceptualization lies the assumption that fixed assets, like the plant and equipment that can be purchased off the shelf by all firms in an industry, cannot be the main source of firms' specific advantage. The OC perspective, therefore, focuses on assets for which no ready market exists.

One crucial idea in the OC perspective is that a firm's capability can only constitute a firm-specific advantage if it is impossible or hard to imitate (Barney 1991). For instance, a particular set of routines and skills can lose their value if they support a type of competence that no longer matters in the marketplace, or if they can be readily replicated or emulated by competitors (Teece et al. *op. cit.*). The issue of imitation and replication is extremely important because it reflects the ability to move the firm-specific advantage to another setting. Replication involves transfer or redeployment of competence from one geographic place to another. As the routines and skills that support this competence are more or less embedded in an organizational and human context, it is often difficult to replicate them in another place without replicating the wider context to some extent. However, given the extent to which they are embedded in the firm, even the understanding of what all the relevant routines are that support a particular firm-specific advantage may be limited. Replication and transfer is, therefore, often impossible without transferring certain key members of staff. Or, as quoted from an interview by a senior manager of Xerox, 'You can see a high performance factory or office, but it just doesn't spread. I don't know why' (Szulanski 1995).

Similar to internalization theory, the OC perspective also maintains that the degree of tacitness of knowledge imposes certain difficulties (Polyani 1957). But while the internalization theory focuses the impact of tacitness on transaction costs, the OC theory highlights the impact on transfer possibilities by replication. In particular, the OC perspective deals with the difficulty of moving a capability from one setting to another without losing its value. The risk of such a decrease in value occurring is higher the more embedded the capability is in its original setting, and the less well understood this embeddedness is. An organizational capability is, by its very nature, not owned by any specific individual, but is embedded in complex social interactions and team relationships within an organization (Granovetter 1985). It cannot be systematically coded and it can be transferred only through a significant degree of direct social interaction (Erramilli et al. 2002).

What more specific implications does the adoption of the OC perspective have on our view of foreign direct investments and the multinational firm? Three different implications of the OC perspective for the theory of foreign direct investment will be suggested below.

**Transacting an Asset or Moving a Capability?**

By definition, foreign direct investment is equivalent to setting up an operation in another country. The traditional logic behind the strategy of foreign direct investment is predominantly to 'do more of the same', that is, to replicate what the firm does in the home country. Within an OC perspective, this strategy involves replicating the true nature of the firm-specific advantage, rather than just producing the same product. This implies applying the same routines, organizational processes, individual competence, and so on, in the new setting as is already applied at home.

An example may help to illustrate this idea. A Swedish producer of cutting tools for industrial use has developed a system that enables each of its customers to obtain the most efficient use of a specific tool in their production processes. The system includes routines explaining how to interact with engineers in the customer firm and is highly dependent on the personal skills of the Swedish cutting tool producer and of its customers, skills that have developed over time. The competitive advantage of the firm, therefore, is considered to be this system, rather than the products as such.

The firm intends to expand into the British market. Owing to the need for intensive, interactive contacts with customers, the firm realizes that the operation, including the production of different qualities of cutting tools, must be physically located in Great Britain. Because of the importance of replicating the system in the new market, the firm also realizes that the design and control of the system must be handled by the British firm itself, including involvement of engineers and marketing people from Sweden. Different forms of collaboration with local firms, such as other producers of cutting tools, distributors and agents, are deemed impossible. The firm, therefore, takes the cumbersome road of establishing its own business from scratch, even though it does not possess all the necessary institutional knowledge about the new market.

This case illustrates how, in certain cases, there are insurmountable difficulties in moving and replicating a highly embedded capability without also moving critical parts of the context in which the capability has been developed. The important observation here is that the decision to make the foreign direct investment does not reflect difficulties arising from negotiations between the firm and a local counterpart concerning the transaction of a single asset. What it reflects, instead, is the difficulty of separating a capability from its context and restoring it in a new context without decreasing its value. By controlling how the facilities supporting the capability are designed in the new setting, its value is preserved. A foreign direct investment occurs. So, when compared with internalization theory, the OC perspective offers a different explanation for why foreign direct investments are made (Madhok 1997).

**Foreign Operations as a Combination of Capabilities**

In contrast to earlier theories, the OC perspective emphasizes how exploiting a firm-specific advantage often requires the combination of capabilities controlled by different agents. For instance, a firm can possess a unique capability concerning how to produce a product in an efficient way, but lack the necessary skill to market the product in a specific country. An extension of the business in the country typically involves a combination of idiosyncratic market know-how, embedded in the local market, and production know-how, embedded in the home country and the local firm. The more embedded the market know-how is in the local context, the more difficult it will be for the investing firm to incorporate the necessary know-how in its own organization. Some sort of collaboration with a local partner may be required. Again, an example may serve to illustrate the point. A company manufacturing glass bottles in Sweden tried to expand its business into the large German market. The company considered its main competitive strength to originate in the so-called 'cold end', that is, the final stage of the production process, including an elaborate system for packaging glass bottles into paper boxes. The company estimated that this strength could be profitably exploited through sales to large German brewers. After some preliminary investigation of the German market, the company discovered that the industry transactions were dominated by close and long-term relationships between brewers, glass producers and distributors. The industry was also characterized by close personal links through memberships in different industrial associations. The company realized that it neither possessed the necessary market know-how to enter the market, nor could it acquire such capability in a short time. Thus, a collaboration in which the Swedish company's production technology was combined with the market know-how of a Germany company active in the relevant business sector was deemed necessary. The first step was to collaborate with one of the main distributors.[1]

To summarize, the OC perspective stresses that a foreign direct investment decision is not solely dependent on the investor's intra-company capability, but also on capabilities outside the firm. Or, expressed otherwise, foreign direct investment is not only a question of the diffusion of knowledge from one place to another, but of the *combination* of knowledge (Madhok 1997).

**Foreign Direct Investment and Value Creation**

The OC perspective maintains that every firm must sustain and develop its core competence (Prahalad and Hamel 1990). This has an implication for how foreign direct investments can be interpreted. Sometimes such an investment is made not to exploit a firm-specific advantage, but to develop one. For instance it has been argued that investments by multinationals in certain areas are made with the specific intention of tapping into the knowledge of that area (Cantwell 1994; Malmberg and Sölvell 2002). The investment takes on more of a listening role, or an opportunity-seeking role, rather than being a way of exploiting a firm-specific advantage already owned by the investor. Thus, it is more of an 'asset-seeking' strategy than a 'market or efficiency-seeking' strategy (Dunning 1993). For instance, foreign investments in Silicon Valley have often been claimed to be of this category. The OC perspective actually claims that it is impossible to make a clear distinction between the exploitation of capabilities and the creation of capabilities. This implies that an analysis of a firm's foreign investment must include both aspects. A specific foreign investment can reflect an intention to benefit from a firm-specific advantage by trying to carry out 'more of the same' abroad. But it can also reflect an intention to learn and develop new competences by investing in a new context. In the latter case, the creation of value is more important than its exploitation. The OC maintains that in every firm there is a mixture of value exploitation and value creation activities. More importantly, every individual foreign venture will probably contain both intentions, although to varying degrees. Therefore, advocates of the OC perspective argue that interpreting a foreign direct investment as an act of economizing on transaction costs is too narrow. A firm may choose to invest in an operation with high transaction costs if the value consequential to that operation is even higher. Or, expressed differently, the long-term revenue side of a foreign adventure must be considered as well as the cost side. This may explain why, even where a seemingly high degree of tacit knowledge is involved, there can sometimes be a preference for collaboration with external partners rather than for investing in wholly owned subsidiaries. Value creation, not cost efficiency, is the crucial element in the OC perspective.

## EVOLUTIONARY THEORIES OF THE MULTINATIONAL FIRM

As discussed above, a crucial issue in the OC perspective is the ability to replicate capabilities. The main concern, in this respect, is that such replication is often impeded by geographic and cultural distances, differences in business logics and, above all, by an inability to divorce the capability from the context in which it was originally created. It is difficult to transfer routines and skills from one place to another. Evolutionary theories of the multinational firm, rooted in the OC perspective, address the transfer issue more specifically.

**The Kogut and Zander Evolutionary Theory**

One such theory was launched by Kogut and Zander during the 1990s and 2000s (Kogut and Zander 1992, 1993, 1995a, 1995b, 1996). Like internalization theory, it supposes that multinational firms are superior for the simple reason that they, as firms, possess certain characteristics. In contrast to the latter theory, though, it is claimed that this is not because the firm is a hierarchy, but because it is a 'social community'.

In line with the OC perspective, Kogut and Zander's evolutionary theory looks upon the multinational firm as a repository of knowledge. This knowledge is primarily embedded in the competence of individuals and in the routines and principles of work within the firm. In that sense, the theory is even more 'sociological' than the OC perspective through its emphasis that knowledge is dependent on individuals. Thus, the knowledge is considered to be 'social knowledge' primarily. The boundaries of the multinational firm demarcate qualitative changes in the reservoir of social knowledge because common identities are developed within the firm. Owing to these common identities, together with routines and 'higher-order principles', it is much easier to transfer information and know-how inside the multinational firm than between independent firms. This is a kind of 'sociological' advantage that the multinational firm possesses, which is quite different from the internalization advantage through hierarchical control.

One assumption made in the theory is that individuals tend to identify themselves with a certain group and develop similar views on things and similar 'codes' of communication. These tendencies are strengthened when there is some similarity in the backgrounds, education, occupation, areas of expertise, and so on, of the members. The common identities developed in such groups will, more or less by definition, facilitate the transfer of knowledge between individuals or subgroups in a profound way. The transfer will be further improved by the routines and organizational principles that are developed over time in the group.

By equating the multinational firm with a group, a social community, Kogut and Zander claim that the most obvious advantage of such a firm is its ability to combine knowledge from different geographical places through transfer. It is much easier to transfer knowledge from one subunit to another within the multinational than it is to transfer the same knowledge from a subunit to a firm outside the multinational. The main reasons are that the subunits are likely to be more familiar with one another, have more experience from earlier knowledge exchanges, share the same views on their goals and strategies, have developed channels for passing on information, be integrated through the use of common routines, and so on; that is, their identities have more in common. Or, as expressed by Kogut and Zander, 'the coherence of the firm is the notional consistency of its business as understood by its members, and for that matter, outside investors and consumers' (Kogut and Zander 1996, p. 514). This advantage becomes more salient, the less codifiable and teachable the know-how to be transferred is.

Kogut and Zander do not deal with the issue of whether a firm in general and the multinational firm in particular can be considered to be one social community rather than several such communities. By claiming that 'a social community is called a firm', they avoid that problem. However, in real life, it is questionable whether firms like ABB or General Electric can be treated as one homogeneous community. Consequently, the extent to which the knowledge transfer advantage pertains when the knowledge has to straddle several social community borders is not clear.

It is interesting to observe that although the Kogut and Zander theory has a strong intellectual connection to OC theory, in stressing that a firm is a 'repository of knowledge' with a combinative capability, it is also strikingly similar to internalization theory. Like the latter theory, a sharp distinction is made between what is inside the multinational firm and what is outside it. Inside the firm there are communication channels, routines, shared views and common experiences arising from knowledge transfer. Outside the firm, only (temporary) transactions exist. This is quite distinct from the general OC theory that emphasizes the need to combine knowledge inside the firm with what is outside. Or, expressed differently, Kogut and Zander do not offer an explanation for why, when extending their foreign operations, multinational firms sometimes prefer joint ventures, strategic alliances, licensing or other forms of cooperation with other firms.[2]

**Cantwell's Evolutionary Theory**

Foreign operations in terms of different forms of cooperation with other firms, though, are of crucial importance in other evolutionary theories on the multinational firm. The most well-known version is suggested by Cantwell (Cantwell 1989, 1991, 1994; Cantwell and Piscitello 2000; Cantwell and Santangelo 2000). The main idea is not that multinational firms are superior because they are social communities but because they are geographically dispersed networks of production units. This network offers the multinational firm access to a variety of different, local, capabilities which it can use to develop its core competence. Accumulating technological competence over time through the interplay between these location-specific advantages linked to the different subunits and the multinational firm's 'original' core capability, is the essence of value creation in the modern multinational firm. In this sense Cantwell's theory becomes more of a theory about evolution (of competence) in multinational firms than Kogut and Zander's theory. The latter theory focuses primarily on certain organizational advantages of the multinational firm but less on how these advantages develop over time.

In contrast to Kogut and Zander, Cantwell's view implies that the multinational firm's external environment plays an explicit role in explaining how the core capability is created and developed. In principle, the main reason for the variety in terms of capabilities that the geographically spread production network offers, is the difference in the subsidiaries' environment. The characteristics of these environments, in terms of the 'knowledge content', as well as the type of relationships between the individual subsidiary and its environment, become crucial. Joint ventures, strategic alliances or other forms of cooperation between the individual subsidiary and other firms in the environment are natural mechanisms for 'extracting' knowledge from the environment. Accumulating technological competence through different forms of cooperation, therefore, becomes a natural element in a foreign direct investment theory.

## THE OC PERSPECTIVE AND THE SOCIETAL ROLE OF THE MULTINATIONAL FIRM

The OC perspective contains a different approach compared to Hymer's market power concerning the conceptualization of the core of firm-specific advantage. The latter approach is intellectually rooted in industrial organization theory, which means that the market position of the multinational firm is of particular interest, as well as the actions the firm can undertake to create and strengthen its position vis-à-vis its competitors. Entry barriers, the threat of substitution, the bargaining power of buyers and suppliers and rivalry within an industry determine the inherent profit potentials of an industry and of subsegments of that industry (Porter 1980; Teece et al. 1997). Rents from the firm-specific advantage flow from privileged positions occupied in the market by certain products. This primarily concerns monopoly rent at the industry level.

The rents stemming from the firm-specific advantages as perceived in the OC perspective are mostly entrepreneurial rents (Teece et al. 1997). This difference between the two perspectives is fundamental for the views they adopt on the societal role of multinationals. In the market power perspective, the multinational firms' monopoly rents can have a negative impact on consumer welfare, whereas in the OC perspective, this is certainly not the most obvious conclusion. On the contrary, the OC perspective implies that firms have to enjoy market imperfections if they are to have the time and resources to develop new capabilities. This is a Schumpeterian view in which an emphasis is put on the exploitation of firm-specific competences to address the changes in the environment (Schumpeter 1947; Nelson and Winter 1982). In a world of perfect competition, there would be no opportunity to develop new capabilities. From a welfare point of view, therefore, multinational firms' advantages, in terms of their organizational capabilities, are not a threat to society and its consumers, but a necessity.

Another difference between the market power approach and the OC perspective is that between exploitation and creation. In Hymer's model, the multinational firm typically exploits an advantage abroad. In the OC perspective foreign direct investment involves an act of creation of firm-specific advantages by combining the investor's capabilities with local capabilities. Knowledge transfer, not diffusion, is the key term. This means, for instance, that while Hymer is concerned about the 'law of uneven development', the OC perspective stresses the role of the multinational firm as a vehicle for the transfer of innovations from one country to others. Therefore direct investments made by multinational firms in, for example, underdeveloped countries will be beneficial for these countries as they gain in knowledge as a result of the investments.

Hymer argued that, 'to equate (multinational firms' growth) with technology and scientific development is mystification' (Hymer 1971,

p. 153). Advocates of the OC perspective would probably strongly disagree. In the evolutionary theory, for example, it is claimed that (multinational) firms are the most efficient instruments for knowledge development owing to their ability to combine knowledge from different places and to develop new knowledge. Similar to internalization theory, the evolutionary theory offers no real possibility to question the social role of the multinational firm. Furthermore, as the multinational firm constitutes the most efficient way to economize on transfer costs, its existence is also optimal for the society concerned.

In his critical examination of the multinational firm, Hymer pointed at the relative size of the multinational firm as the basic problem, rather than the simple fact that they exist because of market imperfections. He was aware of the Schumpeterian argument that unique resources and capabilities must exist for innovative behaviour to occur at the firm level. His concern, though, was the risk that at some point these resources and capabilities might be applied to strengthen the firm's market position, rather than to develop new innovations. Such a risk does not seem to be of any concern to the advocates of the OC perspective.

Inherent in the OC perspective, especially apparent in evolutionary theory, is the tendency to portray a harmonious knowledge-based society. In such a society, the multinational firm is perceived as an efficient vehicle for the transfer of knowledge across borders. There is no room to take into account any diseconomies of the knowledge sought and transferred in the multinational firm. Transfer efficiency can only be assessed – if it is assessed at all – in terms of the aims of the firm. Thus a firm producing and transferring dangerous chemicals can be very efficient in its own terms, but not when considered from the perspective of society. The multinational firm may facilitate knowledge transfer across borders, but from a societal point of view it is not apparent that all types of transfer will be beneficial. The OC perspective offers little help with the analysis of this problem (Ietto-Gillies 2012).

## WHAT DOES THE MULTINATIONAL FIRM LOOK LIKE IN THE OC PERSPECTIVE?

In Hymer's view, multinational firms are primarily strong hierarchies in which the headquarters has the ultimate power. He also claimed that control is implemented through a differentiation of management into three levels: the strategy level, the tactical level and the operational level. How the headquarters' control of the lower levels is actually carried out, though, was not an issue of great concern for Hymer. He simply assumed that the headquarters has the ultimate control.

The advocates of internalization theory also assume that multinational firms are hierarchies, but in contrast to Hymer they adopt a much more elaborate view of the control issue. The control from above must be efficient so that transaction costs are eliminated. Therefore, the tendency of lower levels to cheat and shirk must be curtailed by different administrative systems. Internalization theory deals with the problem of information asymmetry. It is assumed, though, that this can be handled by designing the organization so that subordinates fulfil the goals of the headquarters.

Internalization theory offers a distinct instrumental and mechanical view of the multinational firm as an organization. It is an instrument for the headquarters' intentions and strategies. It is mechanical in the sense that the formal characteristics of the organization are emphasized and the employees of the organization are perceived, above all, as an issue of control and not as a resource in itself.

The OC perspective adopts contradictory views of the multinational firm in many ways. Firstly, the view is much more organic and sociological. Although routines, 'higher organization principles' and administrative systems play a crucial role, the people in the organization, as individuals, are also highly important. In the main, the core capabilities of the multinational firm are a mixture of the firm's organizational processes, developed over time, and its employees. The employees are assumed to be holders of a large part of the knowledge on which the firm-specific advantage is based. Individuals are primarily treated as resources, not as sources of control problems. The perspectives are also sociological in the sense that the multinational firm is conceptualized as a group of individuals rather than as a production function or a system of machinery and equipment.

Secondly, the perspective is much more lateral than hierarchical. The idea that the directives flow downwards and the information passes upwards, which is typical for both Hymer's perspective and internalization theory, is substituted by both lateral and vertical exchange of know-how between individuals and subunits. This exchange is facilitated by the administrative processes that have developed over time in the organization.

Despite these differences the OC perspective, like the knowledge-based view in general, implies that the headquarters has a 'parenting advantage' (Foss 1997). Such an advantage means that the headquarters has a superior ability to decide which value-creating activities to support and which intra-organizational knowledge sharing to establish. As a matter of fact in many studies in this tradition the possibility of the headquarters executing authority over knowledge-creating processes is a necessary condition for the knowledge-based firm. Conner and Prahalad, for instance, claim that the firm is created as a result of the fact that 'the managers' understanding (present and future) is believed to be of superior value compared with corresponding elements of the employees' (Conner and Prahalad 1996, p. 480). Because of differences in employees' knowledge, the headquarters' authority is supposed to be a crucial factor. The headquarters' ability to combine heterogeneous pieces of knowledge by executing authority from above (and not its ability to deal with transaction costs and opportunism as in the Coordinating multinational) is the main reason why firms exist.

Even if the headquarters and its parenting advantage play an important role in most writing within the OC perspective the headquarters is notably absent from Kogut and Zander's evolutionary theory. Their view implies that the multinational firm is more like one big 'happy family'. It is a model of harmony and common interests rather than of conflicts and partial interests. The formal organization, including the issuing of orders by the headquarters, is substituted by the intentional exchange of knowledge between 'equals'. The implementation of the headquarters' strategies is almost reduced to a matter of nurturing shared identities and supporting the development of capability at different levels. The somewhat extreme view adopted in internalization theory whereby human beings are considered to be 'cheaters and shirkers' is substituted by a similarly extreme perception of them as 'altruistic' beings with no interest in maximizing their own interests at the cost of the organization as a whole. At the very least, in Kogut and Zander's approach self-interested behaviour is kept in check by the common identity of the individuals in the multinational firm.

It is not clear whether they claim that every single employee in a large multinational firm is committed to this shared identity. There is no discussion about the existence of a dividing line between those sharing a common identity and those who do not, except for the notion than different specialties can have different identities owing to their particular specialization (Kogut and Zander 1996, p. 513). It is perhaps fair, though, to conclude that when the identity concept is applied, it is implicitly limited to higher echelons of the organization: top management, division managers and, perhaps, the subsidiary managers. What a less comprehensive commitment on the part of the large number of employees working at lower levels would mean for the possibility of the multinational firm functioning as a social community is not addressed.[3] This is problematic because the idea of the multinational firm as a repository of knowledge cannot be meaningfully constrained to a small group of managers. It must include a larger group of employees. In that sense, Kogut and Zander's perspective contains two somewhat contradictory models: a sociological model in which the multinational firm is considered to consist of a dynamic group of knowledgeable and cooperative individuals; and a model about leadership executed by a small and homogeneous group of managers (Forsgren 2008).

## SUMMARY

The OC perspective suggests that the concept of a firm-specific advantage, which plays such an important role in both Hymer's approach and in the internalization theory, must be conceptualized in a different way. Firstly, it is proposed that the concept of firm-specific advantage is more closely linked to the specific firm and the uniqueness of its resources. Secondly, there is a symbiotic relationship between the creation and the exploitation of a firm-specific advantage. Thirdly, the uniqueness of the firm is stored in the minds of people, including the management, rather than in physical facilities. Fourthly, the firm-specific advantage exists throughout the entire multinational firm. Fifthly, firm-specific advantage is about 'know how' as much as 'know what'. Sixthly, firm-specific advantage is as much about value creation as it is about exploitation.

According to the OC perspective, the firm-specific advantage is basically a capability for which no market exists. This capability is 'ingrained in the walls of the firm' and is, therefore, difficult to separate from the firm itself. It is linked to the managerial and organizational processes in the firm, through the firm's routines, current practices and history. As a result, the replication and transfer of the capability is often impossible in the absence of transfer of key personnel.

The OC perspective has certain implications for the way in which one looks upon foreign direct investment. One logical argument for these investments is that of doing 'more of the same abroad'. Within an OC perspective, this implies applying the same routines, organizational processes and using the competence of the same individuals in the new setting. In many cases, this means that there are insurmountable difficulties to moving and replicating a highly embedded capability without moving critical parts of the context in which the capability was developed. In the OC perspective, therefore, the decision to carry out a foreign direct investment does not reflect the difficulty of negotiating a contract with a potential foreign counterpart, but difficulties in imparting a capability from the firm itself. In short, therefore, the OC perspective offers another explanation for why foreign investments occur to that given by internalization theory.

The OC perspective also explains why other modes of operation than foreign direct investment are sometimes made. Exploiting a firm-specific advantage abroad often implies combining the focal firm's capability with capabilities in the possession of other agents. Thus, it is necessary to engage in collaboration with an agent, in a joint venture, strategic alliance, and so on, even in situations when the internalization theory would predict that the firm had to internalize through a foreign direct investment because of high transaction costs.

The OC perspective emphasizes that every multinational firm must sustain and develop its core competence. Thus, foreign direct investments are often made not to exploit a firm-specific advantage, but to develop one. For instance, foreign direct investment can be made to 'tap the knowledge' in a certain country. The OC perspective suggests that in every multinational firm there is a mixture of value exploitation and value creation. More importantly, every individual foreign venture will probably be entered into with both of these objectives, although to varying degrees. A preference for engaging in collaboration with a local partner rather than a foreign investment with 'full' control of the venture may reflect an ambition to pick up new knowledge rather than to exploit existing knowledge. The OC perspective, especially Cantwell's evolutionary view on multinationals, offers a better explanation for such behaviour than the internalization theory.

In Kogut and Zander's perspective the multinational firm is conceptualized as a 'repository of knowledge', and as a 'social community' with a common identity. The barriers to knowledge transfer are, therefore, argued to be less within the multinational firm than outside it or between the firm and its environment.

While the monopoly rents of the multinational firm were of major concern for Hymer, the OC perspective maintains that firm-specific advantages primarily produce entrepreneurial rents. Consequently, the multinational firm has to enjoy market imperfections to get the time and resources to develop new capabilities. From a welfare point of view, therefore, a multinational firm's advantages are not a threat to society and consumers, but a necessity. Multinational firms are also considered to be the most efficient form of knowledge transfer. Therefore, the OC perspective does not offer any obvious reason to question the societal role of the multinational firm.

While the internalization theory adopts a distinct instrumental and mechanical view of the multinational firm, the OC perspective implies a much more organic and sociological view. In the main, the core capability is a mixture of the multinational's organizational processes, which have developed over time, and its employees. Individuals are primarily treated as resources, not as sources of control problems. The directives passed downwards and the information flow upwards, which are typical for both Hymer's model and the internalization theory, are substituted by both vertical and horizontal exchange of know-how between individuals and subunits.

In most writing about the OC perspective the headquarters has a crucial role due to its 'parenting advantage', that is, its supreme ability to decide which value-creating activities to support and which knowledge transfer to carry out. In fact, this ability is a prerequisite for the existence of the firm.

In Kogut and Zanders evolutionary theory the role of the headquarters is less clear. They perceive the multinational firm to be more like a 'happy family'. While the internalization theory takes some account of the potential conflict in interests between the headquarters and the employees, assuming that these can be solved by efficient monitoring, this problem is more or less absent in Kogut and Zander's analysis. The 'cheaters and shirkers' of internalization theory are substituted by 'altruistic' individuals with no intention to maximize their own interests at the cost of the organization as a whole. Consequently, and contradictory to the knowledge-based view in general, the headquarters' execution of authority in the value-creating processes is of limited importance.

## NOTES

1. After some years the company had acquired its own market know-how about the German market, which made it possible to establish its own production plant and sales organization. This case illustrates some basic elements in the so-called Uppsala internationalization process model, which will be treated in greater depth in Chapter 6.
2. Kogut and Zander's view implies that the main advantage of the multinational firm is its ability to economize on transfer costs. Like internalization theory, therefore, the argument is essentially one of cost efficiency. Consequently, a reasonable conclusion to draw from Kogut and Zander's theory would be that multinational firms are created because activities located in different countries are coordinated under the same roof to reduce transfer costs. The difference between this conclusion and the conclusion reached with the transaction cost argument in internalization theory is quite subtle.
3. Perhaps the most obvious case of a common identity can be found among top managers in different multinational firms, rather than between top managers and employees within a particular multinational firm, similar to the way that Hymer looked upon control in the multinational firm (see Chapter 2).

# 5. The Designing multinational: a tale of strategic fit

## INTRODUCTION

In the preceding chapters, three different views of the multinational firm have been presented. The difference between these perspectives has been highlighted. But there are also certain similarities that need to be pointed out.

First, one common trait is the sharp distinction between the multinational firm and its environment. In the internalization theory this is especially obvious, and must necessarily be so, because the dividing line between the market and the firm is fundamental to the theory. If there were no distinction between the market and the firm, there would be no internalization theory. But in Hymer's market power approach and in the OC perspective, too, the dividing line between the firm and its environment is quite sharp. In the former theory, the immediate environment is comprised of real and potential competitors. These competitors play a role in the theory in two ways. First, if the concepts of market imperfection and firm-specific advantage are to be used, the relation between the multinational firm and its competitors must be defined. Second, as we argued in Chapter 2, Hymer's view also includes an element of market collusion between competitors. By joining forces, the multinational firms are able to reduce competition, extend their market power and conquer the world.

In the OC perspective, the focus is on the creation and diffusion of knowledge as a resource that is unique to a firm. Apart from the fact that the theory recognizes that foreign direct investment can include an element of collaboration with local firms, and that a capability runs the risk of being imitated by competitors, the environment is peripheral to the theory. The main issue is what is going on inside the firm, in terms of value creation and transfer. The multinational firm's environment is more or less reduced to an unspecified background against which the value creation activities inside the firm are modelled.

We have argued that the OC perspective adopts a more developed view of the nature of the firm-specific advantage and how it arises. However, similar to Hymer's approach, as well as to the internalization theory, firm-specific advantage is almost entirely an intra-organizational phenomenon. More importantly, the knowledge on which the firm-specific advantage is based is supposed to be entirely controlled by the firm itself. Very little is said about resource dependencies to external actors, nor is it treated that knowledge is largely developed and stored in relationships with other firms rather than inside the firm itself.

Therefore, it is fair to conclude that the three perspectives in general tend to represent a closed rather than open system (Scott 1981). The interaction between the environment and the firm merits only a rudimentary treatment. Very little is said about the extent to which, for instance, the environment plays a role in the establishment of the multinational firm. According to the internalization theory, the multinational firm arises because firms need to internalize activities located in different countries. The influence from the environment, in terms of, for instance, the customers, suppliers, governments or other stakeholders, is not part of that story. Instead, this is a story about internal efficiency, rather than strategy. In the OC perspective, the efficiency, which was perceived in terms of cost, has been replaced by efficiency assessed in terms of value creation. This change in focus, though, does not mean that the interaction with the environment gets a more central role. Instead, the model is still one where efficiency is considered to be more important than strategic behavior as a way to deal with the environment.

Neither of the approaches considered so far dealt with the impact of the environment explicitly. Maybe more importantly, there is no room for variation in the organizational solutions as a consequence of differences in tasks and environments. All multinational firms encounter the same problem and the solutions are the same. In Hymer's theory, the organizational solution includes a strict hierarchy with vertical information channels and with clear separations between the strategic, tactical and operational levels. In the internalization theory, the solutions can vary because of variations in the information asymmetry between the headquarters and the subsidiary. But the degree of information asymmetry and the solutions proposed do not seem to have any relationship with the environment. The environment is brought into the analysis in the guise of market failure, not in terms of variation in the environment. In the OC perspective, the environment is an element to the extent that knowledge transfer can also include exchange with external actors. But there is limited consideration of how differences in the environment and tasks influence the existence and organization of knowledge transfer. Knowledge transfer is a good thing for all multinationals, irrespective of type and business.

There are other perspectives, though, that place the environment of the international firm at the center of the analysis. Common to these views is the assumption that the multinational firm can be understood as a phenomenon only if the characteristics of its environment are analysed explicitly. We will take a closer look at three such perspectives that have played prominent roles in the field of international business research. Although they have a similar aim in involving the environment more explicitly, they are radically different on many points. The first is rooted in contingency theory, the second in business network theory and the third in institutionalization theory.

Historically, the contingency theory approach comes first. Let us see what this theory offers us for our understanding of the multinational firm.

## THE MULTINATIONAL FIRM AND THE CONTINGENCY THEORY

The contingency theory approach emerged at the beginning of the 1970s as an attempt to deal explicitly with the environment as a decisive factor for the way in which the multinational firm should be conceptualized. The approach was rooted in the 'contingency theory'. This is a theory that tries to 'open up' the organization and formulate propositions about how the environment impinges on the strategic behaviour of the firm. Expressed succinctly, the assumptions underlying contingency theory are the following:

1.  There is no one best way to organize a firm.
2.  Not all ways of organizing a firm are equally effective.
3.  The best way to organize a firm depends on the nature of the environment to which the organization must relate (Scott 1981).

These assumptions challenged earlier theories that had tried to identify some general principles that were applicable to all times and places. It was argued that earlier theories overlooked the vast diversity of existing organizational forms and failed to recognize the great variety of tasks undertaken by organizations. But, of equal importance is the assumption that organizing matters: depending on the environment and the task, one form of organization can be much more beneficial for performance than another. The nature of the organization's environment, therefore, plays a crucial role in the theory. The underlying idea is that attaining high performance requires a fit between the environment and how the activities are organized within the firm. Another (implicit) assumption made in contingency theory is that the fit is achieved by the organization adapting itself to the environment, rather than vice versa.

The development of a contingency view was inspired by Chandler's study of 70 US corporations (Chandler 1962). From this study, Chandler concluded that as a firm changes its strategy for products and markets, and consequently meets other environments, it has to change the basic structure of its organization. Thus, there is no single best way to organize the firm; everything depends on the task at hand.

## THE APPLICATION OF CONTINGENCY THEORY ON THE MULTINATIONAL FIRM

In a seminal study of US American multinationals by Stopford and Wells, it was concluded that the development of a firm from a one-product, domestic firm to a multi-product or multi-market firm will force it to change its organizational structure gradually to enable it to handle the challenges involved in the different phases of this development. In their study, they concentrated their analysis on the way the firm copes with its international adventure through the formal organization. Their analysis dealt mainly with the 'timing of structural change' (Stopford and Wells 1972, p. 63). Thus, for example, they argue that early in the development of a firm's foreign activities, foreign business is handled by a separate unit, the international division. This division usually has the same status as the other divisions, irrespective of whether the structure is of a functional or a product-divisional type. If the firm follows a strategy of foreign expansion, this organization will gradually become increasingly inadequate. Communication problems between the international division and the other divisions will arise. For instance, product divisions have no incentive to transfer information about their product development activities to the international division. As a matter of fact, the international division can be seen as a competitor by the product divisions. Furthermore, when the foreign venture expands by introducing more products and/or more countries, the international division will lack the necessary product and/or country expertise.

Thus, at a certain time in the foreign expansion, the multinational firm is forced to change its organization so that it can handle its business more efficiently. In line with Stopford and Wells's study, this change can take one of two different directions. If the most dominant form of expansion is in terms of products, rather than a geographical expansion, the firm will structure its divisions in such a way that they correspond to the products marketed worldwide. If, in contrast, the expansion is primarily geographical, the firm will adopt a structure that corresponds to the geographical areas in which it is active. If the expansion, in terms of products and geography, is equally dominant, Stopford and Wells suggested that the multinational firm needs to apply a structure that can handle both dimensions at the same time: a matrix structure.[1] The relationship in the multinational firm between strategy, in terms of product diversification and foreign expansion on the one hand, and a suitable organizational structure on the other, is illustrated in Figure 5.1.

**The Transnational Solution**

Another illustration of how the multinational firm adapts its organization to the business environment is the classification suggested by Bartlett and Ghoshal (1989). They argue that in industries in which adaptation to different conditions in national markets is crucial, multinational firms have to choose a 'multinational organization' model. The operations abroad are seen by the headquarters as a portfolio of independent businesses, a kind of decentralized federation. In industries in which the main competitive advantage consists of centrally developed new products that are exploited in several national markets, the multinational firm will take on an 'international organization' model. In comparison to the former model the

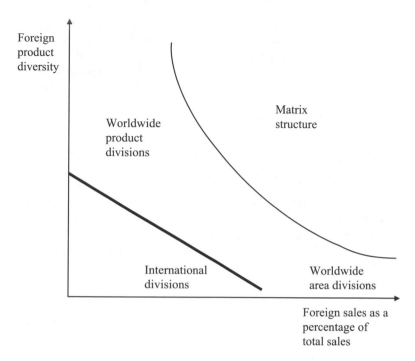

Foreign
product
diversity

Worldwide
product
divisions

Matrix
structure

International
divisions

Worldwide
area divisions

Foreign sales as a
percentage of
total sales

*Source:* Egelhoff (1988).

*Figure 5.1* *Stopford and Wells's model of the relationship between
strategy and organization structure in multinational
firms*

subsidiaries are more tightly controlled by the headquarters and are
first of all seen as appendages to the parent company. In industries in
which economies of scale and standardization are possible to exploit
due to homogenization of customer tastes the successful multinational firm will adopt a global organization model. In such a firm all
strategic resources and decisions are centralized to a few hubs and
the subsidiaries are under tight control by the headquarters.

Although Bartlett and Ghoshal argue that the different forms
reflect different needs due to different business environments, and
in that sense are equally efficient but in different contexts, they also
imply certain inefficiencies. For instance, when resources and capabilities are consolidated at the centre, as in the global organization

model, the subsidiaries have neither the ability nor the motivation to respond to local market needs. With dispersed resources and decentralized decision-making, as in the multinational organization model, subsidiaries can respond to local needs, but the fragmentation of activities will inevitably lead to inefficiencies due to lack of coordination and knowledge transfer between subunits. Bartlett and Ghoshal therefore maintain that the modern efficient multinational has to develop a structure that acknowledges the importance of both local responsiveness and flexibility, and the need for global coordination and economies of scale. Their solution is the 'transnational organization' model (Bartlett and Ghoshal 1989). In such a multinational firm the resources are dispersed but interdependent and the subsidiaries have a certain degree of autonomy at the same time as they are integrated in a worldwide operation. New products and processes are developed jointly and shared worldwide. Such an organization is, simply speaking, a solution that is supposed to contain all the advantages of the other structures without suffering from any of the assumed disadvantages.

**Stopford and Wells's Study and European Firms**

Stopford and Wells's study deals with how US firms change their organization as a consequence of their internationalization. It can be argued that a similar pattern can be traced when it comes to European firms. Historically, though, there is a distinctive difference between US and European firms when it comes to the beginning of the internationalization process. The reason for this is the difference in the size of the home markets. The large domestic market open to US firms meant that they generally started their foreign expansion relatively late, and often made the initial step abroad over the border to the culturally similar market offered by their neighbour, Canada. European firms, on the contrary, had to go abroad much earlier because of their limited home market. In the former case the American firms had a formal structure corresponding to the needs of their home market, for instance in terms of product divisions, and the international division became a natural complement to this structure when the foreign expansion took off. For many European firms, the foreign expansion was already part of the strategy from their earliest expansions, which meant that the headquarters took a very active part in the foreign business abroad. As a result of this, much more direct, but often very informal, links were established between the headquarters of the firm and the foreign subsidiaries, often called a 'mother–daughter structure' (Franko 1976). This led to certain problems when, later, the multinational firm wanted to change its overall organization to either a global product or an area division product. The foreign subsidiaries were used to having direct communication links with the top management, and therefore often resisted having to conform to a new structure in which they only had indirect links to those at the highest level. This conflict was often described as a battle between the 'king of the country', the subsidiary manager, and the 'king of the product', the global divisional manager.

**Information Processing and Strategic Fit**

Already at this stage some fundamental differences can be recognized between the application of contingency theory to the multinational firm and the perspectives presented in Chapters 2–4. In particular, contingency theory deals much more with the interplay between the multinational firm as an organization and its surrounding environment. In the other perspectives, in contrast, limited attention is paid to how the change in the environment, occurring as a result of a change in strategy, affects the internal life of the multinational firm. The fact that a multinational firm can be more or less dispersed in geographical terms, in terms of its products, or by being in different stages of its internationalization process, does not affect how the firm is organized in, for example, the internalization theory. Thus, either the firm internalizes transactions across borders, thereby becoming a multinational firm, or it does not. There is no room for different degrees of internationalization or any link between the firm's strategy and how it is managed. Maintaining a strict hierarchy and imposing 'behavioural constraints' are what counts, even in large multinational firms with highly dispersed operations. Hymer's view is more or less the same: multinational firms are run in the same way irrespective of their size and geographical dispersion or location.

In contrast, contingency theory, as applied to the multinational firm, places the emphasis on the link between the environment and the 'internal life' of the firm. This is especially obvious in the type of contingency theory that has been labelled the 'information processing view' (Egelhoff 1988, 1993). One basic assumption behind this view is that information is required for efficient decision-making. Therefore, the collection, distribution and evaluation of information about markets, competitors and products are the essence of every organization. Another fundamental assumption is that there is always a difference between the required information processing facing the organization and the available information capacity in the organization. The amount of information processing necessary for efficient decision-making is context-specific. For instance, the larger the number of subsidiaries abroad and/or country markets, the larger the amount of information the corporate headquarters has to handle to make decisions about resource allocations. In a similar way, the higher the degree of change in terms of, for instance, the products and technology or the competitive climate, the greater the need for information processing among the decision-makers. These context-specific factors are consequences of the environment and the chosen strategy. In the information-processing view, these factors are exogenous ones.

The available information-processing capacity of the multinational firm depends on how the firm is organized and managed. For instance, within a multi-product strategy, a global product division structure can handle the information required much better than other structures. If there is a high degree of change in the local markets or in the products, a large part of the information processing needs to be carried out at the subsidiary level. Decentralization of the formal decision-making to this level will, therefore, lead to better decisions being taken. If, on the other hand, the strategy implies a high degree of operational interdependence between subunits of the multinational firm, the information-processing view predicts that centralized decision-making is a more efficient solution.

As can be seen from Figure 5.2, the basic idea behind this view – and contingency theory in general – is that a fit is needed between the strategy/environment and the way in which the firm is managed. The information-processing needs and the firm's capacity to satisfy them are intermediate stages in the model. The extent to which the firm manages to close the gap between the required and the available capacity to handle information, that is to attain a high degree of fit, will determine how well the firm will perform. A low degree of fit will also lead to low performance.

This efficiency criterion is a crucial part of all contingency theory. The theory predicts that, in the long run, no firm can survive if

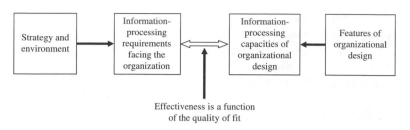

*Source:* Egelhoff (1988).

*Figure 5.2    The information-processing view*

its design, in terms of organizational structure and formal control systems, is inadequate for the prevailing context. A more extreme view, sometimes called 'structural contingency theory', predicts that there is a one-to-one relationship between the context and organizational design (Egelhoff 1988). Only firms adopting an appropriate design, as dictated by the environment, will survive. A less deterministic view, called 'strategic contingency theory', acknowledges that firms have certain degrees of freedom when it comes to the fit between the environment and the organizational design (Larsson 1985). More than one organizational solution might be able to produce the relevant information required for efficient decision-making. For instance, the global product division structure and the area division structure may be equally efficient in a situation when the firm's extensive foreign operation includes many products as well as many regions or countries. However, the strategic contingency theory would propose that, in such a situation, a multinational firm that chooses to locate all its foreign affairs in an international division will not survive, at least not in the long run. The gap between what is required and the capacity becomes too great. There is a strategic choice, but within certain limits. The limit is set by a competitive market in which other firms will strive to achieve optimal performance by maximizing the correspondence between the environment and the way in which the organization is designed.

**Centralization and Strategic Fit**

Inherent in the information-processing view is the problem of overload at the top management level of an organization. The view implies that all decisions would be taken at the top level in the organization if it were not for the fact that the top managers would be overloaded with information-processing work. Or, expressed otherwise, the corporate headquarters will give away formal decision rights only to the extent that practicalities force it to do so. The introduction of the divisional structure is intended to address such a situation. The more diversified the multinational firm becomes, the higher the amount of information that needs to be processed to coordinate the R&D, production and marketing of the different products and for the various markets. At a certain point, the work required in handling the information at the top management level becomes overwhelming, so some of it must be distributed to lower levels in the hierarchy. The corporate headquarters is forced to implement the divisional structure as a solution to that problem.[2]

The information-processing view states that there are four primary disadvantages associated with centralized decision-making in a firm: (1) the decision-making capacity of the top management is quite limited and, consequently, is subject to overload; (2) top management frequently lacks specific knowledge about conditions at the subunit level; (3) moving information up and down the hierarchy requires time and tends to delay decision-making; and (4) centralization can have a negative impact on the motivation of subunit managers (Egelhoff 1988).

The view also implies that there are certain contextual factors that drive centralization of decision-making. In general, these factors can be classified into two main groups according to whether they encourage operational interdependence or bring about change. The higher the operational interdependence between different units in the multinational firm, the greater is the need for centralized decision-making. For instance, the Swedish ball-bearing manufacturer, SKF, has production sites in several countries in Europe. Due to economies of scale, each of these factories is specialized in the production of a certain quality of ball-bearings. At the same time, though, every subsidiary is responsible for marketing and selling SKF's entire range in its host country. As a result, there is a high degree of interdependence between the different subsidiaries in terms of the delivery of products, production and marketing plans, and so on. Such a situation calls for decision-making at a level above that occupied by the subsidiaries.

Some degree of interdependence can probably be handled by

introducing certain rules and programmes. But if we consider that the market for ball-bearings is subject to a relatively high degree of uncertainty and change in the various local markets, the information on which the rules and programmes are based tends to become out of date. Exceptions brought about by these changes must be referred up the hierarchy for a decision to be made.

Other factors, though, can cause decentralization of the decision-making. Simply speaking, these factors can also be classified into two groups: the environmental complexity and size of the multinational firm. For instance, in the SKF case above, the difference between the country markets, in terms of the conditions for doing business, the type of customer, the competitive situation and the quality of the different ball-bearings to be marketed, makes centralized information processing more difficult and threatens to overload the top management. Such a situation will force the headquarters to allow some decisions to be made at the subunit level.

The information-processing view also adopts the perspective that the sheer size of the multinational firm will lead to decentralized decision-making. The reason for this is that size directly affects the volume of information that must be processed. Furthermore, as size of the firm increases, the vertical span from the top management to the operating subunits also lengthens. This tends to delay decisions concerning local affairs if they are taken at the top level.

In an investigation of 50 of the largest US and European multinational companies, the centralization–decentralization dimension was investigated and related to factors concerning the environment and strategy, such as operational interdependence, change, complexity and size, at both the company level and the subsidiary level (Egelhoff 1988). The underlying hypothesis was that, in the most successful multinationals, one would expect a high degree of fit between environment and strategy and the formal organization. Companies with a lower degree of fit would not belong to this group of successful companies.[3]

In general, this investigation pointed at two conflicting pressures of fit. At the company level, increases in the strategic or environmental complexity and the pressure, arising from the size of the multinational firm, encourage decentralized decision-making for all subsidiaries, to buffer the hierarchy from information-processing overload. For instance, the more substantial the foreign operations and the greater the diversity of the products marketed abroad, the more the marketing-related decisions were made by the subsidiaries. Similarly, the higher the extent to which the products were modified locally, or differed from one subsidiary to another, the more the decisions about manufacturing were made at the subsidiary level.

At the subsidiary level, on the other hand, certain pressures existed to centralize decision-making. For instance, there was a negative correlation between the extent to which the individual subsidiary was involved in intra-company sales and the decentralization of the marketing-related decisions to the subsidiary. Similarly, a considerable degree of change in the individual subsidiary's context, for example in terms of changes of products or in the competitive climate, tended to lead to less decentralization of the decision-making to that specific subsidiary.

So, all in all, this study demonstrates that the environmental and strategic factors in a particular multinational firm can lead to conflicting pressures concerning centralization and decentralization. For instance, a high degree of complexity in the products and markets will force the top management to decentralize the decision-making to lower levels. This will ensure that the decisions are taken without too much delay, and that they are made by those who possess the most relevant knowledge for the context. But if, at the same time, there is a high degree of interdependency between the different subunits in the firm, there will be a significant degree of pressure to centralize to achieve efficient coordination and to avoid suboptimal decision-making.

A relevant question within the information-processing view, therefore, concerns the relative strengths of these two pressures of centralization and decentralization. In the study above, this was examined by looking at how much of the variation in the dependent variable, centralization/decentralization, was explained by factors of most relevance to the company as a whole and factors of greatest importance to the subsidiary, respectively. Or, expressed otherwise, is the tendency to decentralize attributable to the complexity and size stronger than the tendency to centralize brought about by the need to respond to change and operational interdependence between subsidiaries? The overall result of this analysis revealed that, while both groups of contextual factors contribute to the explanation of centralization, the complexity and size at the company level are stronger predictors than change and interdependency at the subsidiary level (see Egelhoff 1988, Table 7.5, p. 144). This implies that the most compelling need is to meet the constraints stemming from company-level complexity and size. Or, as Egelhoff expressed it:

> Failure to adequately centralize individual parent–subsidiary relationships in order to achieve better fit with subsidiary-level conditions will only tend to produce suboptimal performance for certain subsidiaries. However, failure to decentralize adequately to fit company-level constraints threatens the entire system or company with suboptimal performance. Thus, the study results suggest that the ability of MNCs to vary centralization from subsidiary to subsidiary to better fit local conditions and information-processing requirements is severely constrained by the ever present danger of information-processing overload at the company level. (Egelhoff *op. cit.*, p. 152)[4]

## Formal Control Systems and Strategic Fit

In addition to the overall organizational structure and the locus of formal decision-making, the formal control system used by the headquarters to monitor subsidiary performance is an important part of 'organizational design' in contingency theory. The formal control system deals with the extent to which the headquarters evaluates and compares data from each subsidiary, through the processing of information on sales, profits, costs and R&D expenditure, including providing feedback to the subsidiaries. According to contingency theory, the context in terms of the environment and strategy will decide which formal control system will be the most appropriate. Accordingly, a high degree of operational interdependence and of change at the subsidiary level increases the need to process information at the level above that of the subsidiary if appropriate coordination within the multinational is to be ensured. Centralization of decision-making is one way to achieve this, but another, complementary, way is to intensify the formal control system exercised by the headquarters. This is accomplished by increasing the amount and frequency of the control information transmitted by the subsidiary to the headquarters, and the amount and frequency of the feedback from the headquarters to the subsidiary. Consequently, a strategic fit between the environment and strategy and the formal control system would imply that when there is a change that increases the subsidiary's interdependence to other subsidiaries, the level of formal control increases. However, similar to the case of centralization, pressures exist that decrease the level of formal control to avoid an overload of information at the top management level. The higher the complexity at the company level, which is affected by the number of subsidiaries, products and markets and the size of the foreign operations, the lower the level of formal control the headquarters can reasonably exercise over its subsidiaries.

In the study referred to above, the relationship between strategic contingencies and the formal control system was also analysed. The overall result supported the expected relationship between the complexity, size of foreign operations, interdependence and change in conditions at the subsidiary level on the one hand, and the level of intensity in the exercise of the formal control system on the other. Similar to the case of centralization, therefore, there are conflicting pressures influencing the design of the formal control system. Certain conditions tell us that intensive monitoring of the subsidiaries through the processing of information between the top management and the subsidiary is a necessity. Other conditions can be prevalent at the same time telling us that this is not a wise thing to do, or is even impossible due to the overload problem at the top management level.[5] In some instances, intensive monitoring of the activities of the subsidiaries appears to be desirable, but because of the overload on the top management this is not an advantageous path to follow, giving rise to a situation in which there is a conflict between the most desirable course and one that can be implemented on a practical level.

The study also indicates that the relationship between centralization and the level of formal control is a complementary one, rather than one being a substitute for the other. The greater the centralization, the greater the tendency is to rely on a high frequency of information transmission between the subsidiary and the headquarters. One reason for this might be that centralizing the decision-making at a corporate level requires access to the latest information about subsidiary operations. Implementing formal control systems is probably the most economical way to transfer this information from the subsidiary up the hierarchy. Thus, from an information-processing point of view, there is reason for co-variation between centralization and the intensity of formal control exercised by the headquarters (Egelhoff 1988).

# THE MULTINATIONAL FIRM AS A DIFFERENTIATED NETWORK

As demonstrated above, the application of the contingency theory to the management of the multinational firm produces different, and sometimes conflicting, answers as to how the firm is or should be managed. A basic reason for this contradiction is that the environment and strategy forces that lead to increased coordination through centralization and tight formal control are counterbalanced by other environmental/strategy forces that drive decentralization and a less tight formal control exercised by the headquarters. It was demonstrated above that one important factor of the latter kind is the diversity of the subsidiary markets. Subsidiaries within the same multinational differ because of differences in their products, business conditions, size, and so on. These differences were addressed in the analysis above when the overall company level was separated from the subsidiary level in the analysis of the relationship between context-related factors and the design of the multinational firm. However, in recent years, attempts to apply the contingency theory to the multinational firm have stressed these differences at the subsidiary level to a much greater extent. The most prominent of these attempts has been presented by Ghoshal and Nohria as 'The multinational firm as a differentiated network' (Ghoshal and Nohria 1997). The starting point for their analysis is that the multinational firm consists of a number of diverse subsidiaries operating in distinct national environments. Each subsidiary is assumed to present unique exigencies that cannot be adequately addressed by a uniform organization-wide structure like a global product division, or a fixed degree of centralization and a formal control system that is replicated for every subsidiary. Ghoshal and Nohria argued that a model that fails to differentiate between the various control linkages so that they ensure that they correspond to the differences between the subsidiaries' contexts 'does not accurately represent the realities of the business world' (Ghoshal and Nohria 1997, p. 4).

The concept of a 'differentiated network' is used to emphasize that the structure of the multinational firm can be understood as distributed resources linked through different types of relations: (1) the 'local' linkages within each national subsidiary; (2) linkages between the headquarters and the subsidiaries; and (3) linkages between the subsidiaries themselves. Any such network forms a complex structure and Ghoshal and Nohria argue that the multinational firm must be perceived to be exactly such a complex structure. The limitations of reducing such a structure to simple terms, like the average levels of centralization or formalization, is obvious. In their view, attempting to ignore the complexity and heterogeneity inherent in these organizations is to fall into what is called the 'reductive fallacy', the failure of 'reducing complexity to simplicity or diversity to uniformity' (Ghoshal and Nohria *op. cit.*, p. 12).

In their empirical application of contingency theory, Ghoshal and Nohria essentially employ two contextual factors reflecting the differences between subsidiaries' environments: (1) the extent to which the subsidiary's environment is complex in terms of a high degree of competition and the rate of product and process innovations in the local industry in which the subsidiary operates; and (2) the significance of the physical and managerial resources that the individual subsidiary controls. The 'organizational design' factors they consider can be classified into three types: (1) centralization, defined as the degree of formal autonomy the subsidiary enjoys regarding its own strategy and policy; (2) formalization, meaning the degree to which manuals, standing orders and standard operating procedures are employed by the headquarters to manage the individual subsidiary; and (3) shared values, referring to the extent to which the subsidiary 'is in tune with the overall goals and management values of the parent company'.

The similarities between this approach and the information-processing view, as applied by Egelhoff (1988) and presented above, are obvious. The environmental complexity and the level of local resources are crucial factors in Egelhoff's analysis, too, although partially measured by other indicators.[6] Similar to the latter approach, centralization also plays an important role as a 'design variable' and formalization is partly equivalent to the formal control system used by Egelhoff. There are, though, two crucial differences compared to the information-processing view. Firstly, a third 'design variable' is introduced in their model, called 'shared values'. Ghoshal and Nohria claim that shared values are as important as centralization and formalization if strategic fit is to be attained between the environment and the way in which the multinational firm is managed. As a matter of fact, and as will be seen below, this variable turns out to be the crucial element in their model.

Secondly, the differentiated network approach considers only the relationship between the headquarters and the individual subsidiary. There is no company-level analysis, as in Egelhoff's study. The issue of fit is solely a matter of how the individual subsidiary is managed by the headquarters. This implies that the use of centralization and formalization can differ substantially between subsidiaries depending on the differences in their environment.

Apart from these differences, the predicted relationships between the environmental factors and centralization/formalization are strikingly similar to the relationships proposed by the information-processing view. For instance, Ghoshal and Nohria propose that the greater the individual subsidiary's environmental complexity and access to local resources, the more the formal decision-making should be decentralized to the subsidiary. The reasons for this are also essentially the same as those given in the information-processing view: namely, the problem of overload at the headquarters level and the advantage in terms of more information at the subsidiary level. Or, as expressed by Ghoshal and Nohria:

> centralization puts the firm at a competitive disadvantage in situations of high environmental complexity that demand well-formulated responses to rapidly changing market conditions. Local managers may resent direction from headquarters when they feel that they have the best sense of the evolving local environment, especially when these managers have a substantial level of resources at hand. (Ghoshal and Nohria 1997, p. 99)

The proposed fit between the subsidiary's environment and formalization is also similar in the two approaches, although the argumentation behind them differs somewhat. Both approaches suggest that a good fit means a higher degree of formalization of the information exchange between the individual subsidiary and the headquarters when there is a high degree of complexity and resource richness at the subsidiary level. In the information-processing view, the reasoning behind this is that such a situation demands more information-processing capacity at the headquarters level, and the formal control system will provide such capacity. In the differentiated network approach, a similar argument can be found, although in combination with the suggestion that formalization provides a mechanism for the headquarters to 'prevent a resource-abundant subsidiary from freely pursuing an independent course of action while at the same time recognizing the realities of the internal power distribution in the company' (Ghoshal and Nohria *op. cit.*, p. 99).[7]

**Shared Values as an Organizational Design Variable**

Although a correspondence between environment and strategy and centralization and formalization sounds reasonable in theory, its application in reality is another matter. Is it reasonable to conceptualize a multinational firm as a 'fit' structure? One important problem in applying contingency theory in the multinational firm is the diversity of the firm. By definition, the multinational firm consists of several subsidiaries and country markets. If the contexts in which some of the subsidiaries are based call for decentralized decision-making, while others call for centralization, what would the appropriate solution be? As seen above, Egelhoff was dealing with this issue when he contrasted the contextual factors at the company level with those at the subsidiary level (Egelhoff 1988). For instance, a high degree of complexity at the company level (such as in terms of a high number of foreign subsidiaries) in combination with a high degree of operational interdependence between subsidiaries (such as in the form of intra-company sales) produced conflicting demands on the formal organization. Furthermore, if the environment of certain subsidiaries called for a high degree of centralization, while the opposite applied for other subsidiaries, what would the appropriate degree of centralization be?

The information-processing view and the differentiated network approach seem to produce different answers to this problem. In the former, as indicated in Egelhoff's study, the considerations at the company level will take over. If complexity at this level demands decentralized decision-making, an overall system of decentralization will be implemented even though contextual variables for some subsidiaries call for centralization. The result will be a uniform system in which all the subsidiaries are treated in the same way.

In the differentiated network approach, the answer is quite the opposite. The fundamental idea behind this approach is that the subsidiaries should be treated differently by the headquarters. Thus an individual fit is sought in the individual headquarters–subsidiary relationships rather than an overall fit. But how will it be possible to treat the subsidiaries differently? Will a subsidiary accept centralized decision-making and a high degree of formalization vis-à-vis the headquarters if some of its sister units are free to make their own decisions and are subject to much less stringent requirements by way of formal reporting up the hierarchy?

The overall answer to this problem in the differentiated network approach is instilling shared values among the managers of the subsidiary. It is argued that the existence of shared values will minimize divergent interests, emphasize mutual interdependence and lead to consensus. It is achieved through the socialization of managers to ensure that they attain a set of shared goals that shape the perspective and behaviour of the various subsidiaries. The approach suggests that subsidiaries can be treated differently if they share common values. Or, as expressed by Ghoshal and Nohria, 'it is possible, as in a strong family that has several children with different personalities, to have a strong set of shared values and yet different rules for each child' (Ghoshal and Nohria 1997, p. 119).

The term 'instilling' is crucial. It reveals that Ghoshal and Nohria look upon shared values in more or less the same way as centralization and formalization: that is, as a design variable that the headquarters can use to achieve a better fit. The headquarters is supposed to be able to increase (and perhaps decrease) the shared values of managers through the implementation of mechanisms such as selection, training and the rotation of managers, stimulation of open communication between headquarters and the subsidiaries and among the subsidiaries, and so on. The shared values are the glue that keeps the multinational firm together. The more differentiated the firm is in terms of diversity at the subsidiary level, the more important the glue. Shared values reduce the inherent forces of gravity and conflict and, above all, allow the multinational firm to fine-tune its administrative fit in every headquarters–subsidiary relationship.

In the differentiated network approach, the use of networking within the organization is intimately linked to the concept of shared values. By 'networking' what is meant are all kinds of vertical and horizontal contacts between units. In their empirical analysis Ghoshal and Nohria define networking as the time spent on inter-unit committees, teams, task forces, meetings and conferences, as well as the time spent by the managers of the subsidiaries visiting the corporate headquarters. They argue that such networking stimulates the social capital of the multinational firm.

The concept of shared values deals with values, beliefs and goals. Networking is the mechanism through which shared values are achieved.[8] The process that leads to increased shared values is the communication between units stimulated by networking. Ghoshal and Nohria also claim that they find empirical support for the supposition that networking positively affects both vertical and lateral communication.[9]

To summarize, in a differentiated network, multinational personal networking leads to more shared values which, in combination with a high fit in terms of centralization and formalization, lead to better performance. The emphasis on networks as a communication device and on the importance of individual subsidiaries and their different contexts makes the perspective very similar to Hedlund's perspective of the multinational firm as a heterarchy, and Bartlett and Ghoshal's concept of the 'transnational solution' (Hedlund 1993; Ghoshal and Nohria 1997). The latter perspectives stress the importance of inter-unit communication as an integrative device. The personal network is seen as the overriding solution to the problem of managing to adapt to local market conditions and achieving integration of the operations and knowledge across units without leaning (too much) on centralization and formalization. Ghoshal and Nohria point to the 'impossibility of building a fully connected network across all the individuals in the organization' (Ghoshal and Nohria 1997, p. 152). Like the other perspectives above, though, they tend to consider the multinational firm to be like a 'brain', in which every unit is connected to every other unit. The more communication in the brain, the better it is. Thus, the cost of communication is not a big issue in these perspectives.

The differentiated network approach is a tale concerning the difference between subsidiaries in terms of their local environments. But it is also a story about how these differences are handled through a common communication network and shared values. In that sense, the term 'differentiated network' is somewhat misleading. It is not the network that is differentiated. On the contrary, the network is supposed to be the common glue that keeps the differentiated activities connected to each other and reasonably integrated.

## CONTINGENCY THEORY AND THE SOCIETAL ROLE OF THE MULTINATIONAL FIRM

In contingency theory, the basic assumption is that a change in the environment leads to a change in the firm's strategy. The change in the strategy, in its turn, forces the firm to adapt its organization to the new situation in order to survive in a world of competition. When applied to the multinational firm, it has been used as a normative theory about management rather than as a descriptive theory. However, the basic assumption about the relationship between the environment, strategy and organization reflects a rather specific view of the role of the multinational firm in the societies in which it is active, and the contingencies for its existence and upon which its behaviour depends. This is an image of the firm as a victim of the environment rather than a master of it. The environment is the exogenous variable, while the strategy and structure are endogenous variables. In most versions of this model it is recognized that the firm has some strategic choice when it comes to how to adapt to the environment in terms of complexity and change. The relationship between the environment and the behaviour of the firm is not completely deterministic. In addition, it is recognized that the firm's adaptation occurs through a process in which there is necessarily a time lag between the change in the environment and the subsequent change in the organization. But the direction is clear and simple: it is the environment that affects the multinational firm, and not the contrary.

The correlation between the environment and strategy and the structure of the organization is also quite straightforward. Firms that do not adapt to the contingencies in the way the theory predicts will not survive. Thus, contingency theory has a certain resemblance to the so-called population-ecology view of firms, in which the environment 'selects' those firms that, for some reason, have adapted themselves to new situations (Aldrich 1979). But in contrast to the latter theory, the contingency theory does not consider this to be a random process in which some firms are lucky and will survive, while others are not, leading to their demise. Indeed, running a multinational according to the contingency theory is supposed to be a managed process in which the top management is capable of assessing what the environment requires from it and acts accordingly.

Like the internalization theory, the underlying assumption in contingency theory is that competition exists between firms. In the long run, the multinational firm cannot deviate from what the environment requires from it. If it were to try to do so, its competitors would take over the market, because their management would match the environment in a more satisfactory manner. This reasoning is similar to the argument underlying internalization theory: that is, if a transaction in the external market leads to high transaction costs, the multinational firm will internalize the transaction. The reason for this is not only that the multinational maximizes its profits, but also that competition forces it to minimize its costs. But while internalization theory emphasizes transaction costs in the external market, contingency theory focuses on the administrative costs inside the firm. Both theories, though, stress how well the conditions inherent in the environment are matched by the way in which the multinational firm is managed. The existence of competition is what drives the optimization process.[10] If we also consider that the internalization theory is actually concerned with the minimization of the sum of the transaction costs and the administrative costs, then the parallels between the two theories become even more apparent.

Therefore, from the perspectives of contingency theory and internalization theory alike, there is little room to question the societal role of the multinational firm. The environment is a given, and the role of the multinational firm is to adapt to the prevailing situation to the greatest possible extent. Thus, the multinational has no power to affect the environment, for instance through bargaining with governments or other institutions, or by reducing competition through collusion with other firms. Or, at least, this is not an important issue. The implication is that the multinationals that exist are the most efficient ones, including from the perspective of society. Otherwise they would not survive. The theory allows for temporary mismatches as a result of the time lag between a change in the environment and the response of the management. But in the long run, such mismatches must be ironed out.

This 'passive' role of the multinational firm can, of course, be questioned on several grounds. It has, for instance, been suggested that the simple, one-way relationship between environment and the firm should be replaced by an alternative form of logic in which the interplay between the firms' actions and their organization is also able to create a new environment (see, for example, Hedlund and Rolander 1990). In line with this, it has been pointed out that the multinational firm often has a great deal of power over its environment. Or as one author put it:

> the merger process at the end of the nineteenth century when Morgan formed US Steel and the centralization of power that Alfred Sloan of General Motors effected in the 1930s were not necessarily adaptations

to a changing environment. These executives *created* a new environment, and other organizations (and communities, families, and individuals) had to do the adapting . . . the mergers of the nineteenth century were quite uneconomical for the first ten or so years and were brought about largely for stock manipulation. *Someone* benefited, of course, or they would not have gone to all that trouble, but it was not the society, the communities, or even the industry. Given the new form, ways were found to make it work, but that is quite contrary to the model's logic. Much the same analysis could be made of Sloan's structural changes [to General Motors:] society had to adapt to the consequences of them. (Perrow 1986, p. 212)

Another example may illustrate the point. In 1967, the Swedish multinational firm Electrolux started to acquire other firms, both at home and abroad. Twelve years later, the number of firms acquired had reached over 100. Some of those based abroad were large, especially in the white goods sector. This wave of acquisition led to the reorganization of the whole sector in Europe, with far-reaching consequences for the other firms in the industry. A large number of small domestic producers of washing-machines, cookers, freezers, refrigerators and so on disappeared as independent producers. The trigger for this action on the part of Electrolux was not primarily a necessity to adapt to changing environments. It was, above all, a response to the sudden and large increase of nearly 600 MSEK in the company's cash holdings that arose from selling real estate and shares in an American company[11] (SOU 1981, p. 43). The substantial increase in cash was combined with an internationalization strategy that was accomplished through acquisition.

The Electrolux case illustrates two important points. Firstly, even though the strategy adopted by Electrolux produced a considerable change in the environment for other firms in the industry, the change itself was produced by a specific actor and not by the environment in general. Electrolux created a new environment, which other firms were forced to adapt to (if they wanted to survive). Consequently, there is no simple relationship between the environment and the strategy and management of all firms. Secondly, even though Electrolux made a strategic choice that was beneficial to the company, we cannot take for granted that the choice was also beneficial for society, for instance in terms of competition. To some extent, it probably reduced some monopolies enjoyed by domestic producers in different countries. But on the other hand, it increased Electrolux's own market power in the global market. The combined result of this development from a social welfare point of view is difficult to estimate. Anyhow, the contingency theory offers little help in such an analysis.

## WHAT DOES THE MULTINATIONAL FIRM LOOK LIKE IN CONTINGENCY THEORY?

As already pointed out, the crucial concept in contingency theory is design. The organization is formed in such a way that a correspondence is attained between the environment and strategy and the organization. The theory predicts that if the multinational is to perform well, it needs to have the right formal organization and control system. In the differentiated network approach, the issue of designing the organization also includes vertical and lateral personal communication links between individuals and units.

However, the presumption that existing firms are designed in line with environmental requirements presupposes that there is someone who is charged with the realization of the design. This someone must have not only the ability to interpret what is going on in the environment, but also the power to implement changes in the organization in accordance with these changes. Thus, both superior knowledge and superior control are needed. This 'someone' is the top management. In contingency theory, it is not feasible to view the existing firm as an organism formed through a process of developing routines, programmes and structures introduced by many people over a long period of time, resulting in chronological layers of adaptations. The contemporary organization of any multinational firm, with its many subsidiaries, markets and products, may be complicated, but contingency theory assumes that the formal organization can be traced back to decisions ultimately made by the top management. It is supposed to be an instrument for the headquarters.[12]

The headquarters' dominance does not imply that all knowledge is concentrated at the top management level. On the contrary, one fundamental issue in contingency theory is the fact that the top management has a limited capacity to process information. Some knowledge in the multinational firm is located at the subsidiary level and the transfer of all the knowledge to the headquarters could not possibly occur without creating serious overload. This is why the locus of decision-making is so important in contingency theory. The headquarters is forced to decentralize certain decisions to the level where the knowledge is located. However, the theory is very distinctive on one point: the headquarters is able to assess what information the subsidiary possesses that it does not possess itself. On the basis of this knowledge, about what it does not know, the headquarters is assumed to be able to design efficient structures, decision rules and control systems. This is very far from the notion of sheer ignorance: the fact that someone not only lacks knowledge, but also lacks the ability to assess what knowledge they are unaware of (Kirzner 1997). This phenomenon is similar to the concept called 'radical uncertainty' (Goodall and Roberts 2003). In the contingency theory, the headquarters in multinational firms suffer from neither sheer ignorance nor radical uncertainty. The environment may be complex and dynamic, but the top management is supposed to be able to assess what is required from it in terms of designing the organization in a proper way.

Another feature of the multinational firm in contingency theory is the absence of conflicts. There is no power struggle in the multinational firm, either between the headquarters and the subsidiaries, or between the subsidiaries. The fact that a certain type of knowledge is concentrated in a particular subsidiary does not imply that this subsidiary has any special ability to affect the allocation of resources or to manipulate control systems to prioritize its own interests over those of the firm as a whole. At least this is not recognized as an important issue in contingency theory. The differentiated network approach stresses the difference between the subsidiaries in terms of environment and operations. This approach, therefore, deals more with conflicts within the multinational firm than contingency theory in general. But it never becomes a real problem for the headquarters. At the end of the day, the headquarters has the ultimate power to design or to change the organization to maximize its efficiency. No subsidiary is able to resist. Or, more precisely, no subsidiary would wish to resist, for the simple reason that the headquarters and the other subsidiaries have shared values which ensure that the behaviour is coherent and results in striving to cooperate, rather than to battle.

## SUMMARY

Through the application of contingency theory in the 1970s, the analysis of the multinational firm came to be not only more management-oriented, but also more open in the sense that the role of the environment became more visible. The basic assumptions made in the contingency theory are that there is no single best way to organize a multinational and that the best way depends on the specific nature of the environment to which the organization must relate. For instance, it was demonstrated that different stages of the internationalization process required different types of organization structure. As long as the number of products marketed abroad and the proportion of sales abroad are moderate, having a separate division that is responsible for the international affairs is sufficient. When the internationalization becomes more significant, in terms of either the number of products or the number of countries involved, it is more appropriate to implement a structure with a global product division or divisions corresponding to geographical areas.

This story concerns the strategic fit between the environment and the organization. Firms change their strategy, which implies that they are confronted with new elements in the environment. These changes will be a threat to the survival of the firm if it fails to change the way it handles the new situation. The contingency theory tells us how this should be done by adapting the formal organization to the new situation. The concept of 'strategic fit' was born. Even though the contingency theory recognizes that there is some room for strategic choice, in the long run no firm will survive if it does not adapt adequately to the environment. It is a fundamental 'iron law' of strategic fit.

When applied to the multinational firm, there are basically two approaches used in conjunction with contingency theory. The first, called the information-processing view, stresses the multinational firm's capacity to process information about products and markets. There are a considerable number of activities and decisions related to R&D, production and marketing that need to be integrated in a multinational enterprise. The more complex and dynamic the firm's environment is, the greater the amount of information to be collected, distributed and evaluated. Thus coordination at the top level of the multinational firm is crucial. However, at some point in time, this work would overwhelm the top management, causing overload. The top management must therefore find ways to reduce its workload.

The information-processing view treats how the tension between the need for coordination and information overload is solved. The focus is on the balance between centralization and decentralization, and the design of the formal control system. The environmental characteristics to which the organizational features must adapt are complexity, operational interdependence and change. For instance, a high degree of complexity (for example, the number of products) forces the top management to decentralize the decision-making; while changes in the environment might force it to centralize the decision-making.

The second approach is that of the multinational firm as a differentiated network. In contrast to the former approach, the difference in the environments and operations between subsidiaries is emphasized. Consequently, adaptation between the environment and the organization must be carried out at the subsidiary level. The administrative linkages between each subsidiary and its headquarters will be unique. If, for instance, a certain subsidiary's environment is more complex than the environments of other subsidiaries, relatively more of the decision-making must be carried out by that subsidiary rather than by the headquarters. The problem of treating subsidiaries differently is handled by introducing the concept of shared values, in terms of common goals and common interests between the subsidiary and the headquarters. Shared values are presumed to be instilled by the headquarters through the support of vertical and lateral personal networks. They are supposed to ensure that different subsidiaries will be motivated to focus on the interests of the firm as a whole, rather than on their partial interests, despite the fact that they are monitored differently by the headquarters.

The application of contingency theory to the multinational firm means that the firm is primarily a victim of the environment. The environment is the exogenous variable, while strategy and formal organization are endogenous ones. Owing to competition between firms, the multinational firm must attempt to attain a satisfactory balance between the environment and the formal organization in order to survive. Similar to the internalization theory, therefore, there is little room for questioning the social role of the multinational firm. It has no power to affect the environment, for instance through bargaining with governments or reducing competition through market collusion. Rather, the multinational firm has to do what it has to do, and that is also beneficial to society.

Design is crucial to contingency theory. This, however, implies that someone must have the ability to design: the headquarters. This does not imply that all knowledge is concentrated at the top, only that the top management has the ability to assess what information the different subsidiaries possess, which it does not possess itself. There is no case of sheer ignorance or radical uncertainty at the top management level. The top management is aware of what it does not know and has the ability to design the organization accordingly. The organization is an instrument for the headquarters, where conflicts between subsidiaries are absent or handled through the existence of shared values in the multinational firm.

## NOTES

1.  Stopford and Wells's data, though, provided only weak support for the existence of matrix organizations when diversification in terms of both products and areas was high.
2.  This reasoning implies that, if a change were to be made to adopt a strategy involving less diversification, the corporate headquarters would reinstall centralized decision-making.
3.  This hypothesis is related to the so-called population-ecology perspective, which says that only the best firms will survive in the long run.
4.  It should be pointed out that, in Egelhoff's study, only about 25 per cent of the variation in centralization was explained by strategic contingency variables reflecting size, complexity, interdependence and change. It would appear that other factors have an influence on where the formal decisions are taken in the multinational firm. I will return to this issue in Chapter 6.
5.  Similar to the analysis of centralization, the strategic contingency factors only contribute to a limited extent to the explanation of variance in the level of formal control (see Egelhoff 1988, Figure 8.2, p. 167). I will return to this issue in Chapter 6.
6.  While Egelhoff has applied several indicators to measure the difference between subsidiaries in terms of, for example, local product modifications, the degree of interdependence between the subsidiary and the rest of the firm, the size of the subsidiary, the dynamism in the subsidiary's market in terms of competitive climate change, product change and technological change, Ghoshal and Nohria concentrated on just two indicators: the degree of competition, and the significance of local resources. In comparison to Egelhoff's analysis, the latter approach is, in fact, guilty of 'reductive fallacy', rather than offering a comprehensive description of the 'real world'.
7.  In an empirical analysis of a large number of subsidiaries in multinational firms, Ghoshal and Nohria claim that they find some support for the proposed relationships among the top-performing subsidiaries. By also investigating the distance between the 'ideal' and the actual centralization/formalization in low-performing subsidiaries, they find additional support for the underlying idea in contingency theory that how the formal organization in a firm is structured has an impact on performance.
8.  In the differentiated network approach, shared values are basically considered to be a phenomenon occurring in the vertical relationship between the corporate

headquarters and the individual subsidiary, while the concept of networking also includes lateral relationships between subsidiaries. Ghoshal and Nohria do not discuss the possible problem that intensive communication between a group of subsidiaries can lead to 'subversive' activities against the corporate headquarters (in contrast to the 'divide and rule' principle in Hymer's reasoning). All kinds of network are supposed to be positively related to the existence of shared values.

9.  This is hardly surprising as communication, as the dependent variable, reflects the frequency of communication; while networking, as the independent variable, mirrors the frequency of contacts. The risk of a tautology overlap is obvious as they appear to be two sides of the same coin.

10. There is an inherent confusion in contingency theory in the sense that the degree of competition is one of the most commonly used variables for describing the environment. But if there is little competition, contingency theory implies that one would expect less need to adapt to the environment than otherwise. Or, to put it simply, if there is no competition, there is no pressing need to care about the costs.

11. The American company, called Electrolux Corp., had been established by the founder of Electrolux (Wenner-Gren). As Electrolux Group was not able to consolidate the company into the group by increasing its 39 per cent shareholding in the company, it decided to sell the shares.

12. It is interesting to note that there is certain resemblance between the design perspective adopted in contingency theory, and the concept of 'intelligent design' among certain theologians, who claim that nature is so complicated that it must be a result of God's design rather than of evolution.

# 6. The Networking multinational: a tale of business relationships

## INTRODUCTION

In Chapter 5, the relationship between the environment and the multinational firm was brought into the analysis in a more profound way than in Chapters 2–4. In this chapter I will continue to consider the role played by the environment, but in a somewhat different way.

The relationship between the environment and the organization raises the fundamental question of what is inside the firm and what is outside it, and of how these two elements should be conceptualized. For instance, is it appropriate to characterize the pertinent markets of the MNC in general terms, such as their degree of complexity, dynamism, competition, and so on? Or should we identify specific actors in the multinational firm's environment and characterize them according to whether they are customers, suppliers, competitors, government agencies, and so on, in an attempt to understand what the environment is comprised of and the role it plays? Similarly, is it appropriate to characterize the multinational corporation as a deliberately designed instrument for implementing a corporate strategy, or is a coalition model (Cyert and March 1963; Pfeffer 1978), taking into account conflicting interests and the power struggle between subunits, a more appropriate image of the multinational firm?

The different views are, of course, related, because both of them deal with the interaction between the environment and the firm. There is, though, a striking difference between how scholars define and treat this interaction. Scholars who are inclined to characterize the environment using broad concepts also tend to adopt a more instrumental view of the multinational firm. The assumption is that the multinational firm is not only capable of analysing the environment in terms of these concepts, but it is also able to adapt the organization to make it better correspond to this environment, thereby optimizing its overall performance.

Scholars adopting the view that the multinational firm is an arena for conflict and power struggle are less optimistic about this ability. Instead they argue that, in reality, the environment is fragmented, context-specific and, especially for those not directly involved in interactions with the environment, impossible to comprehend in any depth. The impact of the environment on the organization is reflected, rather, in the interests that the different subunits choose to pursue and in the resources they can use in the bargaining process (Forsgren et al. 2005).

In Chapter 5 the former view, the contingency theory view, was presented. In this chapter, an alternative perspective of the relationship between the environment and the firm will be introduced that is more in line with the second view. It deviates from the contingency view in the following ways. Firstly, the multinational firm's relationship with its environment is conceptualized primarily as business relationships with specific actors. Secondly, these relationships do not stop at the border of the firm; external business relationships are included as well as internal ones. From the point of view of the individual subsidiary, there is no dramatic difference between external and internal relationships. They all belong to the subsidiary's business network. Thirdly, this network, in its turn, will have a decisive influence on the role of the subsidiary in the multinational firm. The business network represents an important part of the resources the subsidiary controls, and these resources can be used to exert influence within the multinational firm. This implies that the decisive influence on strategic behaviour is not necessarily the headquarters. Sometimes, the tail can wag the dog.

In the following, a business network approach to the multinational firm will be presented. In the first section I make a short presentation of the business network theory. This theory is then applied to the internationalization process and the multinational firm.

## THE BUSINESS NETWORK THEORY

During the last two decades, a conceptualization of the market has appeared that focuses on specific relationships between actors. At the heart of this approach lies the assumption that suppliers and customers are engaged in long-lasting relationships that they consider to be important for their business. Empirical data related to some 1000 business relationships in European markets showed that most firms operate in markets where a limited number of customers account for a considerable proportion of the firms' sales (Håkansson 1982; Turnbull and Valla 1986). Managers tend to characterize their customer distribution by an 80:20 rule, saying that 20 per cent of the customers account for 80 per cent of a firm's sales. In a similar manner, the majority of the firms' purchases come from a limited number of suppliers.

The business relationships are important as they ensure effective sourcing and marketing, and because they form a basis for the firms' competence development. The business relationships are significant, intangible assets held by the firm. The average age of the relationships in the investigation above was 15 years, but a considerable number of them were much older than this (Håkansson 1982).

Business relationships are established and developed by investing time and resources in promoting interaction between actors. Such relationship-specific investments may include the adaptation of products, processes and routines. Adaptations are made gradually as a consequence of two firms learning about each other's way of performing activities. The relationship-investment processes are often mutual. The business relationships are critical for the firm's business. They are difficult for an outsider to comprehend because they comprise a number of different and complex dependencies, involving technical, logistic, cognitive and economic know-how, which are shared between the parties.

Ties to third parties, such as customers' customers, suppliers' suppliers, competitors and public agencies often condition business in a particular relationship. Consequently, markets are more or less stable networks of business relationships. Firms make investments in such networks. The network is the framework that opens up possibilities for a firm and, at the same time, imposes constraints on its business (Forsgren and Johanson 1992).

## BUSINESS NETWORK THEORY AND THE EMERGING MULTINATIONAL FIRM

In the perspectives presented in Chapters 2–4, the main drivers for firms going abroad and becoming multinational are the exploitation of a firm-specific advantage, in combination with the profit and growth objectives. Internationalization is essentially an 'inside-out' phenomenon. It starts with an asset located inside a firm and implies that the firm employs the same asset in foreign markets. Although Hymer acknowledged the problem of the firm having limited knowledge about the foreign markets that it is expanding into, knowledge about foreign markets as such does not play a major role in his model. Hymer believed that the lack of knowledge about the foreign markets could be compensated for by a firm-specific asset. In the internalization theory, in contrast, knowledge about foreign markets is noticeably absent as an element of importance for the creation of the multinational firm. Instead, internationalization arises through the cost-efficient coordination of transactions across borders. The OC perspective recognizes that the firm-specific advantages can be developed through the combination of assets in the foreign markets. But similar to the other two perspectives, knowledge of the foreign markets is not a particularly prominent issue.

In sharp contrast to these perspectives, knowledge of the foreign markets plays a major role in business network theory. The relevant business network is not only crucial for the firm's business and performance, but it is also difficult for an outsider to gain access to it, or to imitate how it works. Successful entry into a foreign market involves much more than building a factory in a foreign country or writing a contract with a local firm. It requires a basic understanding of the relevant foreign business network for the type of product or service in question and how the network functions. Furthermore, the firm must acquire knowledge about who the important players are in the network and how they are related to each other.

Business network theory essentially assumes that such knowledge cannot be acquired without first-hand experience. Or, expressed differently, the firm must be an insider to be able to fully understand the network and which roles the firm might be able to play. The only way to acquire such knowledge is through direct experience, and the only way to get the experience is to gradually and cautiously enter the foreign market by making small investments.

This is the basic reason why the acquisition of market knowledge is such an important variable in the internationalization process within a business network context. In the 1970s a model addressing the internationalization of firms, the so-called 'Uppsala internationalization process model', was presented. The model suggested that lack of knowledge about the foreign market is the main obstacle to international operations. It also claimed that such knowledge must be acquired through active presence in the foreign market rather than by collecting and analysing data about it (Johanson and Vahlne 1977). In line with the assumption that the knowledge relevant to business is tacit and has a specific character, decision-making and the implementation of decisions involve incremental and cautious steps through 'learning by doing'. The firm postpones each successive step into a certain country until the perceived risk associated with the new investment is lower than the maximum tolerable risk. The perceived risk is primarily a function of the level of market knowledge acquired through the firm's own operations.

The Uppsala internationalization process model is a dynamic model in the sense that the firm's current knowledge about a certain country's market and the investments made in that country will have a decisive influence on the future investments in that market. Thus, this is a model involving path-dependence. Based on the interplay between current market knowledge and decisions about future investments, the model predicts that: (1) firms start and continue to invest in just one or a few neighbouring countries rather than in several countries simultaneously; and (2) investments in a specific country are made cautiously, sequentially and concurrently as the employees of the firm learn to operate in that market. The empirical manifestation of the latter pattern is that low-resource-demanding investments will precede high-resource-demanding ones. For instance, in the majority of cases, the firm will try to export through an independent agent in the foreign market before it considers establishing its own sales organization or commencing production in the market.

Although the business network theory was only in its infancy when the Uppsala internationalization process model was launched, there is a clear connection between the former theory and the latter model. This is manifested in the concept of market commitment, which is fundamental to the model. Market commitment has to do with the extent to which an investment in a market activity has alternative uses. The more difficult it is to transfer the resources to another market, or to find another use in the same market, the higher the commitment associated with the investment. Or, as expressed by Johanson and Vahlne, 'An example of resources that cannot easily be directed to another market or used for another purpose is a marketing organization that is specialized around the products of the firm and has established integrated customer relations' (Johanson and Vahlne 1977, p. 29). This example is as close as one can come to the core meaning of a business relationship in business network theory.

In business network theory, both market commitment and market knowledge have a more well-defined meaning than in the Uppsala internationalization process model. Market commitment is mainly comprised of commitments to specific business relationships in a business network. Market knowledge largely consists of knowledge about business partners' capabilities developed through exchange with these partners. Consequently, the internationalization of a firm is a matter of the investment of time and resources in developing business relationships with specific partner firms in other countries. As a path-dependent process, every step of the internationalization process is based on the firm's existing major business relationships. This network of direct and indirect relationships provides the firm with most of the information on which managers can evaluate business opportunities. The search for such opportunities will: (1) lead it to explore the possibility of developing relationships; (2) encourage it to try to coordinate activities across business relationships; and (3) encourage it to try to generalize what has been learned from the experiences associated with its value-creating relationships to other relationships (Forsgren et al. 2005).

The application of the business network theory to the internationalization process means a change in focus compared with the original Uppsala internationalization process model, in two important respects. Firstly, the concept of a foreign country, in terms of economic, institutional and cultural barriers, is a major element in the latter model. Market knowledge, therefore, is basically treated as knowledge of how to surmount these barriers. The country border plays an important role. In the business network theory, the issue of the country border becomes less important. Instead, the opportunities to establish relationships with unique foreign customers and suppliers come to the fore. The issue is to establish a position in a foreign business network, irrespective of whether this network covers a country, part of a country or several countries. It is the barriers of the network that matter rather than country barriers.

Secondly, the original Uppsala internationalization process model predicts that firms tend to follow the so-called establishment chain: that is, to start with indirect export, then to use agents or distributors after some time and, eventually, to end up with more fully fledged operations in terms of establishing their own sales or production subsidiaries. It is much more difficult to predict the chain of events with the business network approach. It is also, perhaps, less relevant as firms' primary aim is to try to organize their foreign business with the intention of supporting, developing and coordinating business relationships. It cannot be taken for granted that this behaviour will be manifested over time in the establishment chain. The forms chosen by the firm reflect the development of the specific network in which the firm is embedded rather than the development of its knowledge about the country barriers. This leads to forms that are both more variable and less predictable over time.

To summarize, therefore, in comparison to the perspectives put forward in Chapters 2–4, in business network theory the emergence of the multinational firm through foreign direct investment is a gradual process rather than a foreign market entry made once and for all. For instance, in the internalization theory, the choice between using an independent agent or a multinational establishing its own sales organization in the foreign market is a matter of minimizing the sum of transaction costs and administrative costs. Only one of the solutions is optimal. In the business network theory, on the other hand, the two solutions can be seen as different stages in the internationalization process, with one giving way to the next at an appropriate time.

Another important difference between the business network approach and the perspectives presented in Chapters 2–4 is the role of foreign market knowledge. In Hymer's model, a lack of knowledge about foreign markets is the primary reason why the investing firm needs to possess a firm-specific advantage large enough to overcome the shortcoming of inadequate knowledge of the foreign market. In the internalization theory the deficiency of foreign market knowledge is reduced to a matter of the uncertainty in transactions. In the OC perspective, lack of market knowledge may lead to the firm combining its own capability with capabilities of local firms. In neither of these theories, however, is the existing market knowledge the main driver of foreign investment. Rather, it is treated as a static element that is unaffected by the internationalization process. In business network theory, on the other hand, market knowledge is a dynamic element that is affected by the foreign investments made and which affects successive investments. The augmentation of the market knowledge is the main driver for the internationalization process, and consequently, for the emergence of the multinational firm.

## BUSINESS NETWORK THEORY AND THE MULTINATIONAL FIRM

Business network theory focuses on the network of business relationships in which a business actor is embedded. At the start of the internationalization process, we can assume that the business actor is the parent firm that is gradually investing abroad from the home country. The business network in which the parent firm is a part will shape the ongoing internationalization process in terms of how and where the investments are made. After some time, the internationalization process will have given rise to a firm with operations in many countries. Who, then, is the business actor at this stage?

One basic assumption in business network theory is that a multinational firm consists of several business actors rather than just one. Even though the multinational firm, as such, is one legal and administrative unit, operationally it consists of several business actors: the subsidiaries. Each subsidiary is embedded in a specific network of business relationships, which is more or less distinct from the networks of other subsidiaries. Since each subsidiary will identify problems and opportunities in its own business network, it will strive either for autonomy in relation to the rest of the company, or for power to influence the development of other parts of the multinational firm in a way that supports the development of its own business network.

Thus, rather than the aspects presented in Chapters 2–5, the conceptualization of the multinational firm has to include not only the geographical configuration of the assets owned by the firm but also the configuration of the business networks in which the different subsidiaries are embedded. Figure 6.1 illustrates this point.

By far the most common way to explore the multinational firm is to start by considering the multinational firm as a legal entity, and then to investigate whether the subsidiaries are also related through the business they conduct. The underlying premise is the corporate context, that is, 'the MNC triangle' illustrated in Figure 6.1. The actors closest to the subsidiaries are selected on legal grounds rather than on business grounds. This means that some of the subsidiar-

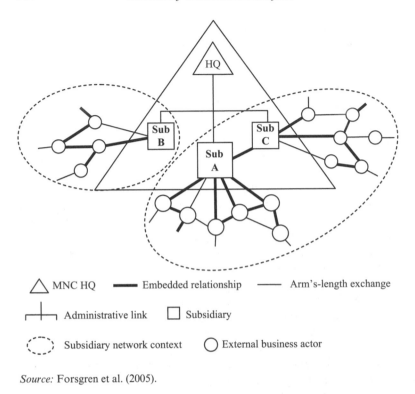

*Source:* Forsgren et al. (2005).

*Figure 6.1    The multinational firm in business network theory*

ies' highly important business partners are treated in a superficial way because they are external to the multinational firm. This is basically the way that the analysis is carried out in, for instance, the differentiated network approach presented in the preceding chapter. The environment of the individual subsidiary is characterized solely in terms of the complexity and degree of competition, and not by business partners. Although the business environment is taken into account, the environment is rather 'faceless'.

The business network theory, in contrast, strives to give the environment of each subsidiary a 'face' by analysing the business relationships surrounding the subsidiary. It is the heterogeneous character of the multinational firm that is emphasized. The subsidiaries are more or less loosely coupled, and are greatly influenced by their business network contexts, irrespective of whether other actors in that network are located inside or outside the multinational firm. From the individual subsidiary's point of view there is certainly a corporate context. But this is only part of the picture. The business network context of the individual subsidiary will be of greatest importance. This context has a profound impact on the subsidiary's business opportunities, capabilities and behaviour. This impact may or may not accord with the intentions of the corporate context.

In Figure 6.1 the business context of Subsidiary B is quite different from its corporate context as all of its business relationships are with external business actors. How it perceives its business opportunities and the demand for future investments is largely shaped by its role in this network, and not only by its role in the corporate context as defined by the headquarters. There is obviously some potential for tension between the business network role and the role defined through its corporate context. How strong this tension is depends on the difference in the perspectives between the individual subsidiary and the headquarters. The dual role of the subsidiary in a multinational firm is stressed much more in the business network theory than in any other theory on the multinational firm.

In Figure 6.1, Subsidiaries A and C are in a somewhat different situation to the extent that their business networks also include a sister unit. The relationship between these subsidiaries is, therefore, of another character than, for instance, between Subsidiaries A and B. A and C are business partners within one and the same network, and not only units within the same legal and administrative entity like A and B. But in this case, too, it is this larger network of business relationships that has a great impact on A's and C's behaviour rather than the group of corporate units (that is, including Subsidiary B and the headquarters).

It should be pointed out once more that the network in the 'multinational firm as a differentiated network' (see Chapter 5) is conceptualized primarily as the formal and informal administrative and communicative links between subsidiaries A, B and C. The business relationships are not included in the network concept, at least not explicitly, and above all, relationships that consist of business exchange with external business actors are not part of the network analysis. In the business network theory, it is rather the opposite case. Networks comprised of business relationships are at the forefront, while administrative and communicative links inside the multinational firm are considered to mirror these relationships to a great extent.

Figure 6.1 also illustrates that the depth of the business relationship is an important variable in business network theory. Some of the relationships are very close in terms of the mutual adaptation of resources and activities, and knowledge exchange (these are called 'embedded relationships' in the figure), while others are of a more arm's-length character. In the former case, the partners are more dependent on each other. This implies that it is difficult for either of the firms concerned to substitute this relationship with a new one. But it also means that the possibility of transferring new knowledge and of solving mutual problems is greater in such a situation.

In arm's-length exchange, the opposite is true. A relationship of this kind is much easier to substitute, but less knowledge transfer is possible and the solving of mutual problems is less likely to occur. Arm's-length exchanges are closer to the conceptualization of a 'market' in neoclassical economic theory, for instance, as presented in Chapter 3 in relation to internalization theory. It should be stressed that the business network theory does not imply that all business relationships are close. Companies will always have a mixture of close relationships and arm's-length ones. What the theory proposes, though, is that by their very nature business activities will produce a certain number of close business relationships. This is a fact that must be accounted for when the behaviour of the multinational firm is analysed.

To summarize, according to business network theory, the multinational firm is active in several business contexts. These contexts can be defined in terms of the business networks in which the different subsidiaries are embedded. The extent that the different subsidiaries are connected to each other is mainly determined by the extent to which the subsidiaries are connected through their business networks rather than through their administrative and legal connections. The underlying theme in the theory is that any firm, including subsidiaries in a multinational firm, will be affected mostly by their business environment rather than by their institutional environment. This is not to deny the importance of country borders or the role of, for example, control systems within the multinational firm. After all, one of the important characteristics of multinational firms is that they operate in several countries and have headquarters trying to monitor the whole group by means of different administrative mechanisms. But the traditional analysis of differences between the countries in which a multinational is active must be complemented with an analysis of the differences between the business networks, and these networks do not have to coincide with country borders. Furthermore, from a control point of view, the headquarters' ability to exert control is challenged by these networks as the networks also influence the behaviour of the subsidiaries.

A specific example may illustrate the last point. In a large Swedish multinational firm, the cost of R&D is enormous. It is therefore of the utmost importance to coordinate the different subsidiaries' R&D to avoid duplication and to achieve large-scale economy. The ability to integrate R&D is assumed to be one of the most critical competitive forces available to the main competitors in the industry. But the driving forces behind product development tend to be local, to a great extent. Thus, specific customers demand special adaptations of the available products that sometimes result in more or less customized R&D activities at the subsidiary level. From the subsidiary's point of view there can be good reason to commence such activities, especially where a large customer is involved. From the perspective of the headquarters, however, what is important is whether or not the results anticipated from such investments will have a wider application in the group as a whole.

One of the largest subsidiaries of the Swedish multinational is located in Italy, which is one of the firm's biggest markets. The subsidiary has always been a very profitable one. As a result of this, the subsidiary has an important role in the group's R&D function, as a developer of both so-called standard applications, that is, applications suitable for several markets; and customer-specific applications, meaning those applications suited to a specific customer only. Customer-specific applications have always dominated in the Italian subsidiary. Changes in the organization of R&D within the group, initiated by the headquarters and intended to increase the proportion of standard applications, have not led to any profound change in this situation. One important reason for this is that almost every request from one very important Italian customer is defined and handled by the subsidiary as a request for a customer-specific application. This is because of the strong and long-standing commercial and social links between the subsidiary and the customer that comprise a close and profitable relationship for both parties. From the subsidiary's point of view, it is more important to maintain and develop this relationship by servicing the customer's special needs than to initiate the development of products that are applicable to other subsidiaries' customers, even though that would be more beneficial for the group as a whole.

This case illustrates that a subsidiary's interest is shaped by its business network. But the case also illustrates that the behaviour of a subsidiary is affected by the depth of its business relationships. The deeper the relationship, in terms of mutual adaptation and a common approach to problem-solving, the greater the impact this relationship will have on the subsidiary's behaviour. The control mechanisms that the headquarters are able to implement can be rather ineffective, and the more so where there is tension between the role of the subsidiary in its business network and its corporate role.

### Control and Influence in a Business Network Context

According to business network theory, each subsidiary operates within a particular network of business relationships, that in turn represents a substantial part of the resources available to the subsidiary and on which it bases its position within the multinational firm. This conclusion applies regardless of whether we focus on relationships with external customers, suppliers, and so on, or on similar relationships with other corporate units. Both types of relationship are part of the subsidiary's network, and the structure and processes within the network define the type of influence that the actors in the network exert upon one another. The more central a subsidiary's position in the network, the greater its chances of influencing the behaviour of another actor. This contention holds irrespective of whether this actor is a corporate or a non-corporate unit: it is business relationships rather than ownership relationships that matter.

This is not to say that other types of relationship do not matter. Influence and control within the multinational firm are also dependent on administrative relationships between units, including the vertical relationship between the headquarters and each subsidiary. For instance, the higher a subsidiary's formal position in the corporation, the greater its chances of exerting an influence on other corporate units. This claim does not only rest on the conception that units higher up in a hierarchy have a legitimate right to give orders to units lower down. It is also based on the assumption that a higher formal position also means better opportunities to survey the environment and to handle uncertainty in an appropriate manner (Hickson et al. 1971). Access to information about the environment means power – something that few would deny.

A pertinent question in business network theory, though, is whether a higher formal position always coincides with more accurate information, and what the information is about. The theory claims that knowledge about the capabilities of other business actors is crucial if the business conducted is to be successful. However, a formal position does not automatically produce such knowledge. Rather, the source can be found in the set of direct and connected business relationships that a unit has with these actors, often built up over a long period of time. These relationships create and support the overall position of the unit within the firm and form the basis of the unit's influence.

Therefore, knowledge about the relevant business network is what matters. Or, to put it another way, any particular unit's influence within the multinational firm is dependent on its knowledge of the strategic resources that the firm has at its disposal. If these resources are largely embedded in business relationships – as is assumed in the business network theory – it follows that first-hand knowledge of these relationships is a crucial source of power. Such first-hand knowledge is created primarily in the course of ongoing interactions with other business actors in the network. Typically, the subsidiaries are involved in these interactions, not the headquarters. First-hand knowledge may be found at the top of the organization, but it has to be acquired in much the same way as at the lower levels. In many cases this is an insurmountable task for top managers in large, dispersed organizations such as the multinational firm.

Thus, while not totally denying the ability of higher hierarchical levels to survey a 'greater' part of the environment, the business network theory suggests that the power of the headquarters rests more on its legitimate right to give and implement orders, than on its superior knowledge. This power should not be underestimated. It is rooted in our culture that a subordinate should obey orders and instructions. Thus, a corporate officer of a multinational firm enjoys considerable power. However, in business network theory, authority does not provide fiat as the dominant or 'last-resort' mechanism of influence. Instead, authority and knowledge about business networks coexist as sources of power. The headquarters typically

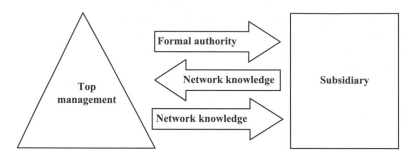

*Figure 6.2    Sources of influence in the multinational firm*

possesses influence through formal authority, while the subsidiary typically earns its influence through its network knowledge. If we recognize that knowledge about business networks also can reside at the top management level, the basic model for influence can be depicted as illustrated in Figure 6.2.

Influence possessed through formal authority is unidirectional and based on the legitimized right to make decisions at the top level and implement the decisions at levels lower down in the hierarchy. Influence arising from network knowledge, in contrast, is reciprocal and is based on access to resources embedded in business networks. The figure indicates that control exerted through formal authority can either be reinforced or counterbalanced by influence attributable to network knowledge (Forsgren et al. 2005). If it is counterbalanced, there is no given limitation to the dominance of a subsidiary within the multinational firm. The net effect may very well be that the higher levels are more dependent on the subsidiary than the reverse, since power based on network knowledge does not differ qualitatively from power based on formal authority. Both sources of power generate dependencies, and which power will dominate remains an empirical question.

To summarize, the business network theory posits that it is normal for a struggle for influence to exist in the multinational firm between the headquarters and the subsidiaries, as well as among the subsidiaries. In that sense, the headquarters is just one player among others. It has to compete for influence with other units within the firm. Furthermore, there are others competing for influence: the external business partners. In an investigation of close to 100 subsidiaries belonging to a number of Swedish multinational firms it was found that there was a significant negative correlation between the average degree of closeness in a subsidiary's business network and the headquarters' influence on the subsidiary's behaviour, as perceived by the subsidiary (Forsgren et al. 2005). This result indicates that, when a subsidiary has a close business relationship with an external business partner, it tends to pay more attention to the interests of that partner, even if these do not coincide with the interests of the headquarters or of the group as a whole.

## The Role of Shared Values in Business Network Theory

The overall picture of the behaviour of the multinational firm in business network theory is as much a story about centrifugal forces as it is about centripetal forces. Owing to the existence of several differentiated business networks in such a firm, and because of the role they play in shaping the interests and behaviour of subunits, there will always be forces striving to push the enterprise in several different directions, rather than only in one. This problem was also recognized in contingency theory (see Chapter 5), but it was assumed that it could, more or less, be eliminated by the headquarters' ability to design the organization efficiently. In the 'differentiated network perspective' the issue of a centrifugal force was addressed more seriously. After all, the basic theme is the difference between subsidiaries that arises as a result of the difference in the markets in which they operate. As shown in Chapter 5, the solution to this problem was to introduce the concept of shared values. Through the existence of common norms and goals, the subsidiaries and the headquarters no longer encounter the problem of centrifugal forces. Several potentially conflicting interests are substituted by one common interest.

The basic idea behind the concept of shared values is that the more the subsidiary and its headquarters are able to view issues in the same light, the more inclined the subsidiary will be to work with other subsidiaries for the good of the organization as a whole. Integration – in terms of, for example, knowledge sharing between subsidiaries – will be stimulated, if not secured, by a high level of shared values.

From the perspective of business network theory, two major objections can be raised against this reasoning. Firstly, the possibility of achieving a high degree of shared values between the subsidiary and the headquarters is seriously overestimated. The specific character of the business networks in which the different subsidiaries are embedded, in combination with the role other business actors play in shaping the interests of the individual subsidiary, are serious barriers to the development of shared values in the multinational firm. In the investigation of 97 subsidiaries in Swedish multinational firms a considerable variation in the level of shared values was found (Forsgren et al. 2005). In only 7 per cent of the cases was the level considered to be very high, and in 30 per cent of the cases it was deemed to be 'medium'. These results indicate that there is reason to be cautious in assuming that the existence of shared values between headquarters and subsidiaries is the norm.

Secondly, business network theory suggests that, even if the level of shared values is high, this is not a guarantee that knowledge will be shared between subsidiaries. Such sharing is largely determined by the relationships between the subsidiaries. It is within these relationships that most of the knowledge sharing takes place. Two subsidiaries can share the same norms and goals with their headquarters, but whether these subsidiaries will influence each other's competence development through knowledge sharing is another matter entirely. In the investigation mentioned above, no relationship was found between the extent to which a subsidiary was involved in knowledge transfer to the rest of the multinational firm and the degree to which shared values were held by the headquarters and the subsidiary. The extent to which the subsidiary was involved in business relationships with sister units, on the other hand, was positively and significantly correlated with such a transfer. This is an indication that business relationships are more important than shared values in understanding integration and cooperation in multinational firms (Forsgren et al. 2005).

## BUSINESS NETWORK THEORY AND THE SOCIETAL ROLE OF THE MULTINATIONAL FIRM

Edith Penrose argued that top managers of large multinational firms are 'non-accountable in the sense that they themselves define the international public interest to be considered' (Penrose 1971, p. 267). This comment is probably as relevant today as it was 1971.

However, Penrose did not take into account the fact that, even if the headquarters of multinational firms are powerful through their exercise of 'economic statesmanship' in societies that their company operates in, exerting power inside the multinational firm is another matter. In business network theory, the multinational firm is conceptualized as a heterogeneous, loosely coupled organization in which no unit, including the headquarters, possesses full control. So, while Penrose observed that top managers, as representatives of organizations with large resources, possess more power in society than is assumed by internalization theory and contingency theory, business network theory suggests that they have less intra-organizational power to control these resources than is assumed in these theories. It should be noted that Penrose's statement and the view adopted in business network theory are not mutually exclusive. Although it sounds somewhat paradoxical, it is quite possible to exert a considerable amount of influence on the political decisions made in a society without having full control over the organization on which this influence is actually based. It is rather like riding a big horse without reins. Such a ride can be impressive, and even intimidating for those in its environment, but it will be full of surprises and irrational events, not least for the rider.

In business network theory the firm is primarily a business actor and not a political one. Even though the business network in which the firm is embedded can include relationships with, for example, governments, public agencies and associations, a typical analysis conducted in line with the theory focuses on relationships with suppliers, distributors, customers and competitors. Thus, the emphasis is put on the business context rather than the political one. However, that does not imply that a business network is, by definition, efficient from a societal point of view. The business network theory is not a functionalistic theory in the same manner as, for instance, internalization theory. What the theory emphasizes is that, in all business activity, relationships arise between actors, and that these relationships must be taken into consideration if one is to understand the behaviour of the actors. But it does not propose that business networks are optimal or do not change. On the contrary, they undergo constant change, for good or for bad, from the perspective of the surrounding society.

In business network theory there is space for questioning the societal role of the multinational firm and its subsidiaries as business actors, although it cannot be said to offer the most appropriate tools for such an analysis. For instance a business network, if it is tightly structured, can function as an effective barrier to the entry of newcomers, more or less in the same way as industry barriers in industrial organization theory reflected in Hymer's perspective. After all, a sharp difference between the insiders and outsiders of a network is an important element in the theory. Such a situation can be detrimental for the efficient use of resources in society and for the development of new technology.

Furthermore, power does not have to be evenly distributed between the members of the network. A network can be dominated by just one firm, which can be highly beneficial for the firm, but it might not be advantageous for society at large. The fact that IKEA is an extremely powerful actor vis-à-vis its suppliers and other actors in its network does not automatically imply that this situation has long-term beneficial consequences for either the network or for the societies in which it or its suppliers operate.

Regarding the societal role of multinational firms, business network theory is rather precise in two respects. The first concerns the multinational firm as a 'global network', that is, a system of more or less integrated subsidiaries.[1] Although the extent to which multinational firms are operationally integrated across subsidiaries and countries is probably overestimated (see for example Kutschker and Schurig 2002), the fact that some sister units have close business relationships with one another influences the political role of the firm. It is often suggested that one of the main political strengths of the multinational firm is that it can move production from one country to another. It has operational flexibility (Kogut 1985). This provides the firm with a strong bargaining position in negotiations with governments about subsidies, or other incentives. The operational flexibility, though, is higher if the subsidiaries are independent from each other than if they are closely linked through strong business relationships. If they are closely linked the multinational firm has applied a system of division of labour. Each subsidiary specializes in a specific activity, but is dependent on other subsidiaries for its operation. In such a situation the multinational firm is much more vulnerable to changes in the localization of its subsidiaries. Consequently, its ability to use operational flexibility in negotiations with governments will be reduced. On a general level, this follows from the simple fact that, in a business network, a member cannot change its operations as though its business were independent from that of the other members. So, the received view of the political power of the multinational firm as a global network (see, for example, Castells 1996) is not indisputable if business network theory is applied.

The other notion concerns the societal role of the multinational firm as a vehicle for knowledge transfer between countries, not least from developed to underdeveloped countries. In business network theory, knowledge transfer between firms becomes a question of the absorptive capacity on both sides. This capacity is much higher if there is a close business relationship between the firms than if there is an arm's-length one. The possibility that, once a specific technology has been transferred inside the multinational firm to a certain subsidiary, it will be received and used by the local business community depends on the business network in which the subsidiary is embedded. If the network consists of arm's-length exchanges, only limited technology transfer into the local community will occur compared to the transfer that would occur if the business relationships were close.

The Lamco case in Liberia may illustrate the point. During the 1960s and 1970s some multinational firms formed a consortium, Lamco, with the intention of exploiting iron ore fields in Liberia. The ore was shipped to steel manufacturers in different countries. Some basic infrastructure was built around the mines, but with very limited involvement of local suppliers in everyday work. When the mines were exhausted, Lamco closed its operation in Liberia and left the country. There were hardly any sustainable spillover effects in terms of gains in technological knowledge made in the local economy. The business network that Lamco built up during the years, which included steel manufacturers and shipping companies, was very beneficial for the operation as such, but it did not include local business actors. This meant that there were almost no identifiable positive consequences for the development of the Liberian economy resulting from the foreign investment.

## WHAT DOES THE MULTINATIONAL FIRM LOOK LIKE IN BUSINESS NETWORK THEORY?

Business network theory suggests that the multinational firm's external markets are less market-like than in the perspectives presented in Chapters 2–5. Markets are not characterized primarily by arm's-length transactions, but by business relationships between specific actors. But the theory also suggests that, on the whole, life inside the multinational firm is more market-like than usually assumed, in the sense that subsidiaries can be looked upon as quasi-firms with their own business agenda. They are related to each other as business partners, and not only as units within the same legal and administrative system.

Implicit in business network theory is the assumption that knowledge about one's own and other actors' capabilities is crucial to gaining an understanding of what actually occurs in the market. This is one of the main reasons for developing business relationships. However, the theory also suggests that this knowledge is widely dispersed and is not passed on to anyone in its totality. Thus, a crucial theme is not only that business actors lack knowledge, but also that they do not even know what knowledge they lack. If one accepts that there are also 'markets' inside the multinational firm, then one has to conclude that every corporate actor suffers from 'sheer ignorance' (Kirzner 1997). Knowledge is incomplete, also, at the headquarters level. And, what is maybe more interesting, the headquarters does not know what the subunits know (and vice versa).

It should be pointed out that this view differs radically from the way in which the uncertainty problem is handled in contingency theory. The latter definitely recognizes the problem of the lack of knowledge of the subsidiaries' operations at the headquarters level and the uncertainty that is linked to this. However, if the headquarters is to be able to design the formal organization and the control system accordingly, it must be able to assess the kind of knowledge that the subsidiary has that it does not possess itself. In a situation of sheer ignorance, this ability is seriously restricted. The headquarters does not know what activities or assets it could be able to control. This makes it difficult to design an efficient control system as required in contingency theory. How can the headquarters decide on the appropriate degree of decentralization of the decision-making to the subsidiaries when it suffers from sheer ignorance?

A fundamental characteristic of the multinational firm in business network theory is that the headquarters is mainly an outsider vis-à-vis the business networks in which its subsidiaries are embedded. If coordination between subsidiaries is one of top managers' major tasks, the difficulties in fulfilling the task are obvious, because knowledge about what other parties involved know is a necessary component of coordinated action (Goodall and Roberts 2003). Note that the main reason for these difficulties is not lack of knowledge about the subsidiaries' operations as such. This can be dealt with through decentralization, the use of integrative organizational forms, performance evaluation, and so on. Rather, the difficulties emanate from the basic fact that headquarters does not know which activities or subsidiaries should be coordinated, or why. If headquarters knows what the subsidiaries do, but not how they do it, it is still possible to accomplish a coordinating role by various organizational means. But if the headquarters does not know what the subsidiaries are doing, or why, then its coordinating role is rather tricky. (Forsgren et al. 2005).

So, in contrast to the theories presented in the preceding chapters, the multinational firm in business network theory is less hierarchical and more loosely coupled. It has a more federative character. Or, as expressed by Ghoshal and Bartlett: 'actual relationships between the headquarters and the subsidiaries and between the subsidiaries themselves tend to be more federative because . . . issues of competency and power tend to be more contested within the MNC and interdependencies among the units tend to be reciprocal as well as sequential' (Ghoshal and Bartlett 1990, p. 607). In this view, the headquarters is considered to be one player among several in the organization. In the federative multinational firm, the headquarters has to compete with different subunits for strategic influence. There is nothing that, a priori, tells us that the headquarters' position will be at its strongest in a situation of conflict between the subsidiary and the headquarters.

So, where other theories talk about the autonomy subsidiaries have, or should have, business network theory also takes into account the actual strategic influence that subsidiaries are able to exert. There are incessant bargaining processes going on in the firm in which different subunits and the headquarters use their power bases to gain influence. The theory also offers a way to analyse these power bases, namely as a reflection of the business network in which the focal unit is embedded. The stronger this network is in terms of knowledge development and profitability, the stronger the position of this subsidiary becomes within the firm. Other parts of the multinational firm will be dependent on the subsidiary's operation. But in line with the theory, the same conclusion can be made concerning the position of the headquarters. Its influence is not equal to its authority based on its formal position. Its capacity to exert an influence within the multinational firm is also a question of its own network and of its understanding of other units' networks.

## SUMMARY

In contrast to contingency theory, the environment in business network theory is above all conceptualized as business networks, consisting of the business relationships between specific actors. The internationalization of the firm from this perspective is a question of successive establishment of a position in a foreign business network. The internationalization process, therefore, is a gradual one in which the acquisition of the business partners' capabilities, developed through exchange with these partners, is crucial. This is a path-dependent process in which every step is based on the firm's most significant existing business relationships.

In line with the conceptualization of the internationalization process, the result of this process – the multinational firm – is supposed to consist of several business actors, rather than just one. Each subsidiary is embedded in a specific network of business relationships, which are more or less distinct from the network of other subsidiaries. Since each subsidiary identifies just the problems and opportunities in its own business network, it tends to strive either for autonomy in relation to the rest of the firm, or to influence other parts of the firm to move in a direction that supports the development of its own business. The underlying theme in the business network theory is that any firm is affected most by its own business environment rather than by its institutional environment, and this is equally true of the subsidiaries in a multinational firm. This is not to deny the importance of country borders or the role of, for example, control systems in the multinational firm. But the theory suggests that the traditional analysis of the difference in terms of countries must be complemented with an analysis of the difference in terms of business networks. These networks do not have to coincide with the borders of the countries involved. Furthermore, the headquarters' possibility of exerting control over its subsidiaries is challenged by these networks as they also influence the behaviour of the various subsidiaries.

The business network theory posits that, in a multinational firm, a struggle for influence between the headquarters and the subsidiary, and among subsidiaries, is common. In that context, shared values, which play such an important role in contingency theory, are of less importance for cooperation and knowledge transfer. What counts is the existence of business relationships between the sister units rather than whether they share the same values and goals as their headquarters or not.

In business network theory, the firm is fundamentally a business actor, and not a political one. The multinational firm is, therefore, analysed in its business context rather than its political context. Furthermore, there is nothing in the theory that tells us that a business network by definition is efficient from a societal point of view. For instance, if the network is tightly structured, it can function as an effective barrier to entry for newcomers. Furthermore, the power among the members of the network does not have to be evenly distributed. A network can be dominated by one firm, which can be highly beneficial for that firm, but may well not be for society at large. The business network theory is not a functionalistic theory in the same manner as, for instance, internalization theory or contingency theory.

## NOTE

1. It should be pointed out that the conceptualization of the multinational firm as a global network has also been applied by researchers within the 'organizational capability' tradition (see, for example, Cantwell and Mudambi 2005).

# 7. The Politicizing multinational: a tale of legitimacy and power

## INTRODUCTION

In the preceding chapter the multinational firm was presented primarily as a business actor. The way in which a firm expands its activities abroad, the structure of the firm, how it is managed and its societal role were all analysed in the context of its business network. The firm's environment was primarily considered to be a business environment incorporating customers, suppliers, sub-suppliers, competitors and research partners. It was a specific environment rather than a general, unspecific one, as is the environment envisaged in internalization theory and contingency theory. The business network environment had a decisive impact on both the external and internal life of the multinational firm.

But business is not only about business networks. It is also about politics. Or, expressed differently, the environment in which the multinational firm operates is also political, and must therefore comply with institutions, legal, cognitive and normative constituencies, and so on. Some parts of this environment are rather specific, similar to a specific customer relationship in the business network, one example being a relationship with a specific public agency. Other parts of the environment are more general and may be 'diffuse', incorporating such diverse aspects as norms and expectations rooted in the culture of a specific country or region. In the same way as the multinational could be analysed as a member of a distinct business network, so it can be conceptualized as a member of political contexts, as a political actor.

The multinational firm's relation to politics and governments is not totally absent from the theories presented in Chapters 2–6. For instance, in Hymer's perspective the ability of the multinational firm to set the agenda and shape its business in negotiations with governments cannot be neglected. In business network theory the 'external' power of the multinational firm is also part of the story.

But in neither of these theories is the role of the multinational firm as a political actor highlighted specifically. It is much more explicit, however, in the approach based on institutionalization theory (Powell and DiMaggio 1991; Rodriguez et al. 2006). On a general level, this approach differs from other theories on the multinational firm in three distinct ways. Firstly, there is an emphasis on the organization as a whole, rather than on specific characteristics such as its market position (as in Hymer's perspective), its hierarchy (as in internalization theory), its core assets (as in the OC perspective), its formal organization (as in contingency theory) or its embeddedness in business relationships (as in business network theory). In that sense, every multinational firm is unique and must be analysed as such. This explains the strong tendency for scholars in this tradition to use case studies in examining enterprises.

Secondly, institutionalization theory points at the possibility that some firms, at least, will take on a life of their own, irrespective of the desires of those presumed to be in control. Basic to this view is the distinction between the rational, means-oriented, efficiency-guided process of administration and the value-laden, adaptive, responsive process of institutionalization. The process of institutionalization is one of organic growth wherein the multinational firm adapts to the strivings of internal groups and the values of the society in which the firm is active. In that process, the top manager of a multinational firm is as much a 'statesman' in a political context as a leader in a business context.

Thirdly, institutionalization theory emphasizes the interplay between the firm and the environment. The ambition to look upon the organization 'as a whole' implies that the 'whole' environment, and not only the 'business' environment in a more narrow sense, is the focus of attention. The environment therefore includes institutions as well as the values and expectations of society. Adaptations to these institutions and values become crucial, and attaining legitimacy in society is an important part of the life of the multinational firm. But the interplay between the environment and the firm is twofold. Not only do firms adapt to society; but society also adapts to large and powerful firms. Or, as expressed by one author in this tradition:

> The environment of most powerful organizations is well controlled by them, quite stable, and made up of other organizations with similar

interests, or ones they control. Standard Oil and Shell may compete at the intersection of two highways, but they do not compete in the numerous areas where their interests are critical, such as foreign policy, tax laws, import quotas, government funding of research and development, highway expansion, internal combustion engines, pollution restrictions, and so on. Nor do they have a particularly turbulent relationship to other powerful organizations such as auto companies, the highway construction firms, the Department of Defence, the Department of Transportation, the State Department, the major financial institutions. (Perrow 1986, p. 174)

## THE INSTITUTIONALIZATION THEORY AND THE EMERGING MULTINATIONAL

In business network theory, the internationalization process primarily requires the firm to invest its time and resources in developing business relationships with specific business partners abroad. It is a path-dependent process in which every step is dependent on the business network in which the firm is embedded at that time. This view of the internationalization process could probably be shared by those using the lenses of institutionalization theory. In line with the latter perspective, business network theory also emphasizes that: (1) history and previous investments have a great impact on the future behaviour of firms; and (2) firms' behaviour cannot be understood without including the specific environment of each firm under consideration. However, the perspectives differ distinctively on two important points.

Firstly, business network theory tends to substitute the concept of country with the concept of the business network. The issue is to establish a position in a foreign business network, irrespective of whether this network covers an entire country, part of a country or even several countries. In contrast, the country, viewed as an institution, and the borders of that country are crucial in institutionalization theory. Countries do not only represent markets and business opportunities, they also represent differences in the legal systems, political contexts, labour and financial markets, business systems, values, and so on. These are crucial factors that have an impact on the possibilities and difficulties of establishing a sustainable presence in a new territory abroad.

Secondly, a related view in institutionalization theory is that the issue of foreign investment cannot be reduced to a matter of establishing a position in a business network. There is so much more for the investing firm to consider, not all of which can be considered business. Politics is involved to a large extent. Or, expressed differently, the foreign investor has to achieve a certain degree of legitimacy in the foreign institutional context. The firm can be perceived as a competent and reliable partner by customers and suppliers, but if it has no or only limited credibility in the political sphere, in the media and among the population in general, the possibility of successfully establishing a position in the foreign society will be severely curtailed (Gebert Persson 2006).

Legitimacy is dependent on how a firm is perceived by society as a whole. This implies gaining credibility in a particular institutional context. Consequently, and in contrast to the Uppsala model of internationalization, entering a foreign market is not only a question of gradual investments being made in conjunction with increasing knowledge about business opportunities. It is also a question of gaining gradual understanding of the explicit and implicit 'rules' related to institutions such as governmental bodies, trade unions, the media, financial markets, and so on. These rules constitute the expectations made of the firm by society. The rules crystallize the expectations society has of the firm, and a firm entering this society has to adapt to these expectations. Therefore, through the inclusion of legitimacy, the prediction of a firm's internationalization process becomes less straightforward than in the Uppsala model. When the attainment of political credibility is a major issue in the establishment of operations abroad, the process of investment can be speeded up or slowed down in comparison to what the Uppsala model predicts. Furthermore, the route taken may be completely different.

Legitimacy is a broad concept incorporating many different aspects. An example may serve to illustrate this. When a Swedish insurance company tried to enter the Polish market for group life insurances, the only way to attain the required level of credibility in the Polish market for group life insurance products was to cooperate with a trade union. A Polish insurance company offering group life insurance was, therefore, started as a joint venture between the Swedish company and one of the biggest trade unions. According to Polish law, though, no trade union was allowed to own more than 10 per cent of the shares in a company. Another restriction was that foreign investors were not allowed to own as much as 50 per cent of the shares in a Polish company. This combination of circumstances forced the Swedish company to invite a third company to participate as a 'window' partner in the project. For various reasons, a forestry company in Poland, with no interest in the insurance business whatsoever, took on that role (Gebert Persson 2006).

The next step in the entry process was to obtain the licence required from the government for this new joint venture. During the application process, though, it became apparent that the government had already issued too many licences, as a result of which a number of the smaller insurance companies were fighting against losses and impending bankruptcy. The authorities, however, mentioned that a Polish insurance company that was not in the life insurance business was in desperate need of capital. In the negotiations, the Swedish company got the impression that the government perceived it to be a potential part of the solution to the Polish company's problem. Or, as one of the managers in the Swedish company expressed it:

> The financial authorities made us aware of the problem (expressing it nicely). One can say that if we had not bought (X) it would probably have taken much longer for us to receive the license. They would of course not do anything illegal or in any other way act inappropriately as Poland had applied for membership of the EU. But, they made us aware that (X) was available to buy and it probably made it easier to receive the licence. (Gebert Persson and Steinby 2006, p. 875)

The application process resulted in the Swedish company acquiring 49.5 per cent of the shares in the Polish insurance company. After some time, the licence application was approved and the sale of group life insurance in Poland could start.

But a new problem immediately emerged that had an impact on how the Swedish company was perceived by society. The partner in the joint venture, the trade union, was heavily criticized in the media in both Sweden and Poland for its connection with the old communist regime and for its conflict with Solidarity, the other big trade union in Poland. The joint venture, therefore, also became a target for criticism, not least by the trade unions in Sweden, but also by a large fraction of Polish society. The joint venture seemed to be in conflict with some basic values of society, and the company was forced to explain its policy and defend its investment in different media in Sweden and Poland. The company deemed it necessary to improve its reputation and image as this critique had had a negative impact on the possibility of selling group life insurances (Gebert Persson 2006).

This case illustrates, firstly, that entering a foreign market is a question not only of establishing business relationships with customers and suppliers, but also of managing to establish the basic support of the surrounding society. The entry process which the Swedish insurance company followed resulted in relationships with two other firms, neither of which had anything to do with the group life insurance business as such, but both of which were necessary for the company to attain the legitimacy it needed if it were to be able to operate in the Polish institutional environment.

Secondly, it also illustrates that there are many aspects involved in obtaining legitimacy (DiMaggio and Powell 1983; Kostova and Zaheer 1999). One is the coercive or prescriptive aspect, composed of regulatory institutions, which imposes itself through rules and laws. In the case study, a government-issued licence was required to establish a business in Poland. Another aspect is the normative one, meaning that a company has to demonstrate that its social values are congruent with those of the surrounding society. The fact that the Swedish company cooperated with a trade union which then suffered criticism from different angles threatened the company's normative legitimacy, and forced the company to take actions to improve its image through embarking on a variety of public relations activities. Thirdly, it was generally accepted in Poland that group life insurance is something that is linked to trade union activities. The Swedish company, therefore, had to cooperate with a well-known trade union to attain what can be called cognitive legitimacy: the adaptation of the behaviour to conform to a norm that is taken for granted in society.

To summarize, in accordance with institutional theory, building up and preserving legitimacy in a foreign country is an important part of the internationalization process. This requires that the multinational firm understands what the institutional context demands of it and what is expected by society. This is as much a form of political activity as it is a business one, in the sense that it involves interactions with authorities and the general public through the use of different media, and not only with business partners.

# INSTITUTIONALIZATION THEORY AND THE MULTINATIONAL FIRM

One of the main characteristics of the multinational firm is that it is a participant in a fragmented or pluralistic context, in which a variety of institutional agencies advocate different patterns of behaviour (Westney 1993). Although this is also relevant for domestic firms, the fact that multinational firms, by definition, operate in different countries makes this even more important. This is the issue of institutionalization theory. It offers tools with which to evaluate the impact of the institutional environment on the behaviour of the multinational firm, as well as the way the multinational firm affects the institutional environment. In the context of the multinational firm, therefore, the difference between institutional environments at the country level becomes the main target for the analysis.

Another main feature of the institutionalization theory is the assertion that organizations are affected by a 'common understanding of what is appropriate behaviour' (Zucker 1983). Firms' behaviour, therefore, is only partly driven by technical efficiency and competitive pressure. Of equal importance is the adaptation to different institutional environments, defined as sets of 'highly established and culturally sanctioned action patterns and expectations' (Lincoln et al. 1986, p. 340). Such environmental isomorphism may come about through coercive, mimetic or normative pressures (DiMaggio and Powell 1983).

In the context of the multinational firm there are three main issues to which the institutionalization theory has been applied. The first of these is the problem of the cross-national transfer of policy within the multinational firm. The second issue is the conflicting pressure for isomorphism at the subsidiary level in the multinational firm, and the third is the role of the multinational firm as a political actor in the different countries' institutional environments.

## Cross-National Transfer of Policy

In Chapter 4, the transfer of knowledge and capabilities was seen as a crucial process within the multinational firm. This is also a major issue in institutionalization theory. In the OC perspective, critical issues were the tacitness of knowledge and the difficulties of separating the knowledge from the context in which it was created, which created barriers to the transfer of the knowledge. The barriers were mainly perceived to be located inside the multinational firm. In institutionalization theory, on the other hand, the barriers and problems are located outside the firm, in the institutional environment. More specifically, the theory deals with the difference between the institutions in the country of origin and in the receiving subsidiary's country. The focus is on understanding complex differences between national business systems through gaining an understanding of the institutions governing the way in which product, labour and financial markets work and the way in which institutional actors relate to one another. Such cross-national differences place various degrees of constraint on the international dissemination of practices within the multinational firm (Ferner et al. 2005).

It has been proposed that a key variable in this context is 'institutional distance' (Kostova 1999). This comprises the differences in the regulatory, normative and cognitive institutions between countries. For instance, there can be considerable differences between countries in terms of their corporate tax policy, people's attitudes to gender issues or knowledge about possible environmental threats. The institutionalization theory predicts that the larger the institutional distance, the more difficult it will be to transfer a practice or policy from, for example, the parent company to a subsidiary in another country. Sometimes such transfer will be carried out through formal adherence to a policy without ensuring complete internalization of the underlying values. In such a situation, the subsidiary is likely to only pay lip service to it. In other situations, a 'hybridization' of the transferred practice occurs, with the danger that the practice becomes significantly reshaped, with a possible loss of the functionality it possessed in its original location (Kostova 1999).

In a study of US multinational firms' attempts to transfer their recruitment policy to their UK subsidiaries, and especially their policy of ensuring 'diversity' of the workforce, it was shown that considerable resistance was encountered from the subsidiaries. Although the subsidiary managers were favourable to diversity as a concept, there was a strong perception that the headquarters' policy was being driven by parochial US problems, that in turn led to initiatives which were inappropriate for the British environment. One UK subsidiary saw the policy as a response to severe racial tensions in US plants and to ensuing litigation. It could not see the justification for the wholesale import of the resulting suite of policies for developing a more inclusive corporate culture in UK operations. Another UK manager complained that the corporate anti-harassment policy referred to bodies like the Ku Klux Klan, which were irrelevant in the British context. Furthermore, monitoring of ethnic groups in the workforce was based on American categories that were inappropriate in the UK (Ferner et al. 2005).

In the study mentioned, it was also apparent that the UK subsidiaries had sought possibilities to resist the transfer, or at least modify it. The transfer process became a negotiated process rather than an 'either–or' one, in which the practices were debated and modified. The subsidiaries were in a position to mobilize resources that gave them power to negotiate the 'terms' of the transfer. To a large extent, these resources emanated from the fact that the subsidiary had first-hand knowledge of the local institutional environment in which the new policy was supposed to be implemented. Not only did institutions in the host country directly constrain the scope for international transfer of policies within the multinational firm, but subsidiary managers' roles as the 'interpreters' of the local institutional environment also gave them power to negotiate the terms of transfer. Subsidiary managers may use their power to deflect a practice from its original function or content, leading to 'resistive' hybridization, or they can engage in ritual compliance, draining the practice being transferred of its original meaning.

To summarize, the institutionalization theory emphasizes the differences in the institutional environments between countries, demonstrating that they represent considerable barriers to the transfer of practices and policies within the multinational firm. Furthermore, these differences can, in their own right, also constitute a power base for the subsidiaries in their negotiations with the headquarters about the transfer terms. Therefore, the institutional environment of the multinational firm induces a politicization of the organizational processes within the firm, which makes it a much more loosely coupled and less rational organization. This stands in sharp contrast to how contingency theory conceptualizes the impact of the environment on the structure of and processes in the multinational firm (see Chapter 5).

## Conflicting Pressures for Isomorphism at the Subsidiary Level

Applied to the domestic firm, the impact of the environment in institutionalization theory is quite straightforward. The theory predicts that there is a strong isomorphic pull from the firm's institutional environment. The firm experiences strong pressure to conform, to 'do in Rome as the Romans do' by conforming to the laws, rules, values and norms in the country, even if this happens to violate its economic efficiency in a more narrow sense. But if the same idea is applied to the multinational firm, the situation is much more complex. The reason for this is quite simply that a multinational firm is comprised of different subsidiaries operating in different institutional contexts. Every subsidiary has, in effect, two distinct environments: one made up of the institutions and firms in its host country, and one consisting of the rest of the multinational firm, including the headquarters and other subsidiaries. In line with institutionalization theory, we can expect that both of these environments exert isomorphic pulls on the subsidiary. It simultaneously faces pressure to conform to the values, norms and 'locally accepted practices' of the host country, and an imperative for consistency within the multinational firm (Rosenzweig and Singh 1991; Blumentritt and Nigh 2002). The latter pressure reflects both the desire to replicate existing organizational features throughout a multinational and the tendency to apply a common control system in the multinational firm. For instance, Procter & Gamble explicitly sought to design each new foreign subsidiary as an exact replica of the US Procter & Gamble organization, in the belief that using exactly the same policies and procedures overseas would lead to the same degree of success (Bartlett and Ghoshal 1989). As far as the control system is concerned, a usual feature is to have a common system for all subsidiaries, for instance a profit-centre system rather than a separate control system for each and every subsidiary.

The interesting point made by the advocates of the institutionalization theory is that this 'isomorphic conflict' in the multinational firm is manifested in a never-ending process, even though one pressure can dominate over the other in a specific situation. If the adaptation to the local institutional environment is given too great a prominence, the multinational firm will run the risk of falling apart as an organization. If, on the other hand, conformity to the corporate system is prioritized too strongly, the multinational firm will risk losing its legitimacy in the different local institutional environments. The problem becomes even more complex when one realizes that there are conflicting pressures, not only on every subsidiary, but also on every function and process within the firm (Rosenzweig and Singh 1991).

## The Political Role of the Multinational Firm

It is probably fair to say that the perspectives presented in Chapters 2–6 pay limited attention to the political environment of the multinational firm and the interplay between this environment and the firm. To the extent to which this aspect has been included in the analyses, there is an explicit or implicit assumption that there is a sharp distinction between the regulating bodies – governments or intergovernmental bodies such as the World Trade Organization (WTO) or EU – and the regulated actor, the multinational firm. With the possible exception of Hymer's perspective the ability of the multinational firm to influence the rules of the game to push them in a direction that is favourable to its business is not a main issue of concern. Implicit in Hymer's perspective is the assertion that multinational firms possess political power, as well as market power. But it is the latter that is at the centre of his analysis.

Institutionalization theory explicitly opens up the political 'box'. In this theory, the spotlight is on the impact the laws, norms and values have on the multinational firm's behaviour, in addition to the 'pure' business or market considerations. In addition to this, however, the theory also points out that the interaction with the institutional environment is by no means a one-way street from the regulators to the regulated (Engwall 2006; Rosenzweig and Singh 1991). Multinational firms are not only reactive, but notoriously proactive. It has even been suggested that the 'liability of foreignness', which for Hymer was an obstacle to foreign direct investment, can actually be an advantage for the multinational firm in its relation with the host country's institutions due to more favourable treatment compared to domestic firms (Edman 2009).

This proactive behaviour can take many forms. One example is to present as positive a picture as possible of the firm's social responsibility in the media and through other official channels, and not only to report on its financial performance. Another is to use persuasion, through lobbying or even in the form of threats, such as stating that the firm will have to move its production to another country for tax reasons unless some condition is satisfied or certain changes are made. The bargaining position of the multinational firm can be quite strong due to its flexibility in reallocating its operations to other countries in response to changes in markets and governmental policies (Rugman and Verbeke 1998).

One sign of the importance of the proactive behaviour is that large corporations create special boundary-spanning units to handle relations with governments, the media and the public. Another sign is the multinational firms' involvement in the regulation and standardization of different business activities, at both national and international level. This is often carried out through membership in corporate interest organizations. At the turn of the twenty-first century, there were around 30 000 international organizations, of which 80 per cent were non-governmental ones. In particular, there are numerous organizations in specific sectors that influence decision-making processes concerning the sector in question. The rules and standards produced are often arrived at in close cooperation with governmental officials and representatives of business and, in particular, the major industrial players (Engwall 2006).

An example is the influence exerted by multinational firms in the WTO negotiations. In the US delegation, the multinationals are especially well represented. The key to this representation is the system of trade advisory committees that bring the public's interests to the US delegation. According to a statement made by the government, these committees must be 'fairly balanced in terms of points of view represented and the functions to be performed'. In a 1991 study by Public Citizen's Congress Watch it was found that, of the 111 members of the committees, only two represented labour unions and there were no consumer representatives at all. At the same time, 92 of the members represented individual companies and 16 represented industry associations. The most important committee, the Advisory Board for Trade Policy and Negotiations, included large multinational firms such as IBM, AT&T, Bethlehem Steel, Time Warner, 3M, Corning, Bank of America, American Express, Scott Paper, Dow Chemical, Boeing, Eastman Kodak, Mobil, Amoco, Pfizer, Hewlett Packard, Weyerhouser and General Motors. The representatives were most often the chief executive officer (CEO) or the chairman of the board (Korten 2001).

In the context of political influence, the issue of corporate social responsibility (CSR) is also of interest. CSR can be defined, broadly, as the efforts corporations make above and beyond the regulations to balance the needs of stakeholders with a need to make profits.

CSR is a question of balancing 'doing well' on the business front with 'doing good' in society (Doane 2005). However, even though most multinational firms put a great deal of effort into issuing social and environmental reports alongside their regular financial reports, it is far from sure that this has altered the overall landscape in a profound way. There are indications that multinational firms are as much regulating the CSR field as they are being regulated by it, and that CSR can also be looked upon as a 'rationalized myth', in terms of a new management trend rather than something that has an actual impact on the firm's behaviour (Sahlin-Andersson 2006).

To summarize, more than any other theory in this book, institutionalization theory deals with the issue of the political role of the multinational firm. Although one basic theme in this theory is that the environment puts pressure on the firm of a non-business character, to which the firm has to adapt, it also applies a more dynamic and interactive approach on this issue by focusing on the ability of the firm to shape the environment through its own political actions. In that sense, the multinational firm is as much an actor in a political arena as it is an actor in a business arena. These arenas are, of course, interdependent. The point, though, is that it makes as much sense to study the game in the political arena as it does to study it in the business arena if we wish to understand multinational firms' behaviour. This is a crucial insight of institutionalization theory.

## INSTITUTIONALIZATION THEORY AND THE SOCIETAL ROLE OF THE MULTINATIONAL FIRM

Some of the theories presented in the preceding chapters include some kind of automatic correction to the size and power of the multinational firm. In the internalization theory, this corrective behaviour stems from the need for the firm to be cost-efficient, which it achieves by focusing on the transaction costs and administration costs. The size of the firm is set so that the sum of these costs is minimized. Therefore, the size of the firm is also cost-efficient from a societal point of view. The theory does not offer any specific reason to bother about monopoly rents due to the ability of multinational firms to shape their environment at the cost of other stakeholders in society.

In the contingency theory the argumentation is somewhat similar. As a result of the competition between firms, those companies that do not attain an efficient strategic fit between the environment and the structure and processes within the firm will not succeed in the long run. Only adaptive firms will survive. Even though there can be a time lag between a change in the environment and a subsequent change in the organization, the common theme is that the multinational firms in existence are the most efficient ones. Competition among firms will ensure this.

In the OC perspective the reasoning is somewhat different. The focus here is on the uniqueness of the multinational firm and on its ability to create and transfer capabilities. In principle, this uniqueness and this ability could lead to a situation of monopolistic advantage that could exhibit itself by one multinational possessing too much market power and exerting too much political power. The theory, though, emphasizes that there are always dynamic forces acting in society when it comes to development of new knowledge. In combination with the possibility of imitation by other firms, this means that there no such thing as a quiet life for any firm in the long run. A firm always needs to be at the cutting edge in order to survive. Consequently, the multinational firms currently in existence are those that have demonstrated a superior ability to create new values in terms of new technologies and products.

The theories above, therefore, include a counterbalance to too much power being exerted by a multinational firm. Institutionalization theory does not encompass such an 'automatic correction'. There is nothing in the theory that leads us to conclude that multinational firms by definition are 'socially controlled'. The theory is quite mixed from a societal point of view. One strand within the theory emphasizes the multinational firms' tendency to adapt to external institutions in terms of rules, norms and values. In that sense, it has a quite passive or reactive role. But as has been demonstrated above, other themes in the theory emphasize that multinational firms can have a much more proactive role vis-à-vis society. These themes leave room for the idea that powerful multinationals can shape the environment in such a way that they maximize their own short-term profits instead of being beneficial for society in the long run. The outcome hinges on the power balance between the multinational firm and the surrounding society. There is nothing in the theory that, a priori, sets a limit on how powerful the multinational firm can be. Each firm and situation is unique.

## WHAT DOES THE MULTINATIONAL FIRM LOOK LIKE IN INSTITUTIONALIZATION THEORY?

One major thought behind the view of the firm adopted in institutionalization theory is that 'things are not as they seem'. Applying this view to the multinational firm is tantamount to trying to look beneath the surface of the organization. For instance, the explanation for organizational behaviour is not mainly found in its function as a hierarchy (as for example in Hymer's theory and the internalization theory), in its formal structure and control system (as in contingency theory) or in its structure of external and internal business relationships (as was presumed in business network theory). Institutionalization theory does not deny that these aspects should be included, but its main contribution is to add all the 'myriad subterranean processes of informal groups, conflicts between groups, recruitment policies, dependencies on outside groups and constituencies, the striving for prestige, community values, the local community power structure, and legal institutions' (Perrow 1986, p. 159). But in line with the theory, this is insufficient. A single process cannot be analysed meaningfully without taking into account the rest of the organization and the other processes going on at the same time. It is its nesting into 'the whole' that gives it meaning. So, simply speaking, the theory advocates that literally everything should be included.

Given this, it is far from clear what the main building blocks should be when the firm is viewed as an organization. In a way it is as much an attitude and a view on methodology as it is a specific model, because of its ambition to consider 'everything'.[1] When applied to the multinational, though, there are certain aspects of the theory that are significantly different from the other perspectives discussed in this book. Firstly, it takes by far the most sociological and organic view of the multinational firm. In line with institutionalization theory in general, multinational firms are as much value-laden institutions as they are rational, means-oriented, efficiency-guided organizations. They may very well exist because they have 'institutionalized' themselves rather than because they offer the most rational and economic solution to a specific problem or demand in society. This stands in sharp contrast to internalization theory or contingency theory.

Secondly, it is by far the most 'open' view of the firm. While contingency theory includes the impact of the environment through rather superficial categories and business network theory focuses on specific external business relationships, institutionalization theory encompasses the entire environment. Compared to other theories, then, it points out that there is a much larger set of factors in the environment that will influence the behaviour of the multinational firm.

Thirdly, the multinational firm as an organization is loosely coupled rather than being a homogeneous and hierarchical entity. The basic reason for this is the emphasis on the importance of the institutional environment. As every country has its own institutions and the multinational firm, by definition, operates in several countries, it follows that the 'typical' environment is extremely heterogeneous. Institutionalization theory predicts that a common way to handle the different isomorphic pulls is to let the various subunits deal with this issue rather than to try to apply a common, corporate-wide solution (Westney 1993).

Fourthly, a characteristic feature of the theory is that it recognizes the conflict at the subsidiary level between two external institutional environments: the local institutions in the host country, and the 'institutions' within the rest of the multinational firm. This conflict is manifested in negotiation processes between the headquarters and the subsidiaries concerning the implementation of corporate rules, values and norms in the subsidiary without violating the subsidiary's position or legitimacy in its local environment. In that sense, the subsidiaries have two 'masters'. This perspective has much in common with the dual role discussed in the business network theory attributable to the tension between the subsidiary's business context and its corporate context.

Fifthly, in institutionalization theory subsidiaries have first-hand knowledge and experience of their local institutional context, which gives them power in their negotiations with their headquarters. Consequently, no one controls the multinational firm entirely and indisputably, neither the headquarters nor any other unit. Similar to the view adopted in business network theory, the multinational firm is as much a federation as it is a coherent body ultimately controlled by the headquarters.

## SUMMARY

The environment of the multinational firm encompasses not only business issues: it is also a political environment. Thus the multinational firm is as much a political actor as a business one. This is highlighted specifically in the institutionalization theory. On a general level, this theory has three main characteristics: it focuses on the firm as a whole, it emphasizes the organic rather than the means-oriented processes within the firm, and it recognizes the interplay between the firm and the environment in its entirety.

Applied to the internationalization process, institutionalization theory differs from business network theory on two important points. Firstly, countries and their borders become crucial because they represent differences in legal systems, political institutions, labour markets, norms, culture, and so on. These factors have an impact on the possibility of the firm establishing a sustainable presence in a foreign context. Secondly, the issue of foreign investment cannot be reduced to one of establishing a position in a business network. The firm is forced to achieve a certain degree of legitimacy in the foreign country, irrespective of its business relationships, by adapting to implicit and explicit rules related to institutions such as governmental bodies, trade unions, the media, industry associations, the general public, and so on. Therefore, the inclusion of legitimacy makes the prediction of a firm's internationalization process less straightforward, but perhaps more realistic, than in the Uppsala process model.

In the context of the multinational firm, there are essentially three issues to which the institutionalization theory has been applied. The first one is the problem of the cross-national transfer of policy or best practice within the multinational firm. This deals with the constraints on transfer arising from the difference in institutions between the country of origin and the receiving subsidiary's country. Key concepts in this analysis are 'institutional distance' and the 'hybridization' of policies and practices (Kostova 1999).

The second issue is that of the conflicting pressures for isomorphism at the subsidiary level within the multinational firm. There is a strong pressure imposed on the subsidiary 'to do in Rome as the Romans do'. Consequently, the individual subsidiary has two environments that it is obliged to take into account: one comprised of the institutions in its host country, and the other being the corporate environment within the multinational firm. Thus, the subsidiary faces simultaneously a pressure to conform to both of these environments. As a result a number of 'isomorphic conflicts' arise throughout the multinational that manifest themselves in a state of flux arising from perpetual bargaining between different interests.

The third issue is the multinational firm as a proactive political player in the different countries' institutional contexts. One sign of such behaviour is that multinational firms create boundary-spanning units to handle their relations with governments, the media and the general public. Another is the multinational firms' involvement in the work intended to regulate and standardize different business activities, at both national and international level.

In contrast to some of the other theories presented in this book, the institutionalization theory does not imply that multinational firms by definition are unquestionably good or superior as members of society. Indeed, the message in this respect is quite mixed. On the one hand, the theory emphasizes the multinational firm's tendency to adapt to the values of the surrounding society. On the other hand, it opens up the possibility of the multinational firm affecting and manipulating the environment in accordance with its own economic interests.

Concerning the multinational firm as an organization, the view of institutionalization theory can be delineated in the following way. Firstly, it is a sociological, organic view of the multinational firm. Secondly, it includes the entire environment in the analysis of the organization. Thirdly, the multinational firm is loosely coupled, rather than a homogeneous, hierarchical entity. Fourthly, a characteristic feature of every subsidiary is that it is subject to pressure from two different environments: the local institutional and the corporate. Fifthly, these pressures represent different interests and power structures within the multinational firm. No one controls the firm entirely and incontestably, neither the headquarters, nor any other unit.

# NOTE

1. Some economists would probably argue that the theory disregards the most important thing, which is how to sell products and make a profit.

# 8. The Multidimensional multinational: concluding remarks

## INTRODUCTION

In the preceding chapters, six different tales of the multinational firm were presented and analysed. Each and every one tells a unique and comprehensive story about the multinational firm as an organization, and about its role in the societies in which it operates. The tales are complex and multidimensional, making comparisons difficult. It is inevitable that any comparison will be somewhat arbitrary and leave out important aspects. Interestingly, they are also very much children of their times. The tale of the Dominating multinational was presented during the 1960s and in many ways laid the foundation for the development of subsequent theories. It can be argued that the view underlying the Coordinating multinational reflects dominant thinking of the neoliberal 1980s, while the Knowing multinational is more related to the view of societies – and of firms – as full-fledged 'information economies' during the 1990s. The story behind the Designing multinational has been around ever since it was presented at the beginning of the 1970s. But the development into the approach known as the 'multinational firm as a differentiated network' has an unmistakable flavour of the 'information economy'. The Networking multinational and the Politicizing multinational can, in many ways, be seen as later reactions against the idea of the all-knowing, information-processing multinational firm.

However, there are interesting differences and similarities in the tales that can be highlighted by comparing certain core dimensions, one by one. The basic theory behind the story is, naturally, fundamental to such contrasts because it sets the playground and constitutes the backbone. It is also illuminating to reflect on what a specific tale would look like when confronted with certain questions about core characteristics of the firm as a phenomenon. For instance, what does any one of these tales say about the critical strength of the multinational firm? Simply speaking, what makes it keep going and growing? How is the firm conceptualized as an organization? Is it an instrument for someone to satisfy certain goals, or an arena for conflict and negotiation between many different subgroups? What is the critical role of the headquarters? What is the possibility for the headquarters to control and influence all events in the multinational firm? How the firm's environment is conceptualized is also of fundamental importance. What does the environment look like? What is the border between the firm and the environment? Which influences which?

A certain perspective also leads to more or less explicit conclusions about the role of the firm as a member of the larger society. For instance, what are the welfare implications of the firm's business activities? Can the firm do well and be good at the same time or is there always an inherent contradiction between the two roles?

## A COMPARISON ALONG SOME DIMENSIONS

In Table 8.1, the six different perspectives of the multinational firm have been compared along some of these dimensions. It should be stressed that the intention of the table is neither to present the complete stories, nor to compare them in their totality. The purpose is, rather, to highlight some crucial differences and similarities.

Firstly, it is obvious that the six tales differ quite distinctively in terms of their theoretical foundations. One of the main differences is between theories that conceptualize the multinational firm as a general phenomenon, and theories that assume that every multinational is unique and must be analysed accordingly. The Dominating multinational, the Coordinating multinational and the Designing multinational belong to the first category. The Dominating multinational considers the firm from the perspective of neoclassical economic theory with the addition that the firm possesses a firm-specific advantage that other enterprises do not have. This tale does not tell us anything about a specific multinational firm or its competitive advantage. The message concerns all multinationals. Even more general in this sense is the story of the Coordinating multinational. The basic message here is that the multinational – as a firm – has certain characteristics that explain why these firms

Table 8.1 Six perspectives on the multinational firm: some core dimensions

| | The Dominating multinational | The Coordinating multinational | The Knowing multinational | The Designing multinational | The Networking multinational | The Politicizing multinational |
|---|---|---|---|---|---|---|
| Source of theory | Industrial organization theory | Transaction cost theory | Organizational capability theory | Contingency theory | Business network theory | Institutionalization theory |
| Core ability as a multinational firm | To exploit a monopolistic advantage in foreign markets | To internalize markets across country borders | To create, transfer, combine and use unique capabilities in foreign countries | To adapt the organization to the complexity and change of foreign markets | To use subsidiary business networks in different countries as strategic resources | To get support from and to influence the international institutional environment |
| Organization view | Hierarchy | Hierarchy | A less hierarchical view implying both vertical and lateral exchange of information | A formal organization supported by 'shared values' | A 'federation' with dispersed power | A complex, 'whole' and value-laden institution |

150

| | | | | | | |
|---|---|---|---|---|---|---|
| Critical role of headquarters | To 'divide and rule' | To apply appropriate behavioural constraints to subunits | Mixed: some advocates emphasize the critical role of 'parenting advantage' of the headquarters | To 'read' the environment and decide on the appropriate organization | One 'player' among others' in the fight for control over strategic investments | To handle politics and conflicts due to different institutional settings |
| Main characteristics of the environment | Local and global competitors | An anonymous market of independent business actors | An anonymous market of independent business actors | Defined as degree of complexity, dynamism and competitiveness | Several environments in terms of the subsidiaries' business networks | The national and international institutions in a broad sense to which the multinational firm is related |
| Welfare implications | Limited competition and market power can lead to severe welfare losses in the societies in which the multinationals are active | Efficient instruments for society to coordinate economic activities across borders | Superior ability to create and transfer new knowledge to foreign countries which is beneficial for society as a whole | Superior ability to identify and implement the most efficient organization, which is also beneficial for society as a whole | Can mobilize large resources and influence markets in line with their own interests; but the control of the resources is incomplete | Can influence policy and institutions in line with their own interests rather than in accordance with the interests of society as a whole |

exist at all. The reasoning is applicable to any firm, except with the addition of the notion concerning multinational firms that different activities sometimes have to be carried out in different countries. This approach offers limited space for a discussion of the difference between multinationals.

The uniqueness of individual multinationals is also of minor interest in the story about the Designing multinational. Multinational firms that operate in a similar environment in terms of industry and geography also become identical in the sense that they develop similar organizational forms and control systems in order to survive. Within that framework, the story does not deal particularly with the character of the individual firm. As we argued in Chapter 5, not even the application of the multinational firm as a 'differentiated network' stresses the difference between individual multinationals. The story is much more about similarities in terms of the existence of personal networks and shared values.

The other three approaches tell a different story. In the Knowing multinational, the unique nature of the capabilities of each and every multinational is the essential message. It is almost impossible to separate these capabilities from the firm that possesses them. They are closely linked to the routines and organizational principles of the individual firm. In the tale of the Networking multinational, the uniqueness of the multinational firm is even more obvious. It is not only the multinational firm as a whole that is unique, but rather each and every subsidiary within the firm, owing to their embeddedness in unique business networks. Finally, in the Politicizing multinational, the core message is that every multinational must be analysed as a 'whole', as a unique case. This approach implies a more or less strong resistance to generalizations about organizations, and therefore also about multinationals.

The basic distinction between the multinational firm as a general phenomenon and as a unique organization is fundamental to the view of its role in society. The Dominating, the Coordinating and the Designing multinational present relatively distinct, albeit contradictory, views. In the first approach they are seen as a possible threat to society, in the second and the third more as efficient instruments for social welfare. The stories make a common supposition concerning the validity of making statements about multinational firms as a group. This is justified because they do not deal with differences and details at the firm level.

The other three stories do that. They stress individual characters to a greater extent, which implies that it is considerably more difficult to state that multinationals are either good or bad. Any benefit or disadvantage to society is dependent on the individual multinational rather than on the concept of 'multinationality' per se. The Networking multinational and the Politicizing multinational do not offer any precise predictions about welfare implications. The stories tell us that they can be advantageous for society, but they can also use their power to enhance their own profits at the cost of other stakeholders. There is nothing in the approaches and the underlying theories that by definition makes the outcome evident, in terms of whether a multinational is of advantage to society or not. One has to consider the individual multinational.

In principle, the same goes for the Knowing multinational. Value creation is presumed to be the main process in the multinational firm, but value creation requires a certain monopoly, which in itself can be detrimental to society under certain circumstances. So, once more, whether the existence of multinationals is beneficial or not is far from a foregone conclusion. However, it is probably fair to claim that the proponents of the Knowing multinational have stressed the good side, in terms of value creation, rather than the bad side, in terms of threat of reduced competition. There is also some reasoning in the tale of the Knowing multinational that seems to argue that multinational firms are necessarily good. The evolutionary theory of the multinational firm and its notion of the firm as a social community is a striking example.

Table 8.1 reveals other main differences and similarities. The view on what a multinational firm is, as an organization, differs quite distinctively. Above all, there is a dividing line between descriptions that assume that a multinational firm is primarily a hierarchy in which the formal organization plays a crucial role, and others that focus much more on the informal, human and complex character of the multinational firm. In the latter category we find the Knowing multinational, the Networking multinational and the Politicizing multinational.

The different perspectives adopted for the organization reflect how the theories look upon the role of the top management in the multinational firm. There is a sharp demarcation between perspectives that assume that the headquarters has the ultimate power and theories that look upon the multinational firm as an arena for conflict in which the headquarters has less than 'full control'. The latter assumption is apparent in the Networking multinational and the Politicizing multinational, while the former is more apparent in the other descriptions. Neither in Hymer's view of the multinational, nor in the internalization theory, is there any doubt about the top managers' ability to monitor the subsidiaries and implement a corporate strategy. Behind the Designing multinational there is basically the same reasoning, although the lack of information at the top management level is an important issue in that story. This problem, though, is handled as a design problem, and the decision to organize in a specific way is made by the headquarters. In all three of these accounts there is no doubt that at the end of the day the multinational firm is firmly controlled by the headquarters.

The tale of the Knowing multinational offers a mixed view of the role of the headquarters. On one hand a dominant perspective of the knowledge-based view implies that headquarters has a 'parenting advantage' (Foss 1997). Such an advantage is based on a superior ability to organize and control the value-creating activities of the multinational firm. Some advocates for the knowledge-based view even argue that the existence of the headquarters is the fundamental reason for the existence of firms (Conner and Prahalad 1996). On the other hand, in many writings the control possibilities of the headquarters are less straightforward than in the Dominating or Coordinating multinational for the simple reason that knowledge is as much stored in minds of individuals as in physical facilities. In some writings, therefore, the role of the headquarters is downplayed. For instance, in Kogut and Zander's evolutionary theory, the role of the headquarters has been substituted by the multinational firm being a 'social community'. If people in the firm identify themselves with the rest of the firm, the development and transfer of knowledge is supposed to be carried out 'automatically', without much communication and coordination by the headquarters. So basically, the tale of the Knowing multinational encompasses everything from a dominant to a more or less absent headquarters.

In the Networking multinational and the Politicizing multinational, intra-organizational power is one of the main issues. In the former, the headquarters is seen as one player among others engaged in a power struggle; whilst in the latter, the headquarters' role of balancing the conflicting views – and sources of power – between different institutional settings is emphasized. An important consequence of this concentration on the role of power – in sharp contrast to the perspective behind the Designing multinational – is that the existing formal organization and routines reflect power structures and not only decisions made at the top level. For instance, decentralization of the formal decision-making to particular subsidiaries is as much a consequence of these subsidiaries' power as it reflects a decision about organizational design made by the headquarters.

Another demarcation line can be placed between the accounts that treat the environment rather superficially and those that place it at the centre of the analysis. But there are also distinctive differences among those that belong to the latter category. In the Designing multinational, the relationship with the environment is quite straightforward. The environment affects the multinational firm. It is a case of one-way adaptation. In the Networking and Politicizing multinational, the relationship between the environment and the firm is more interactive and complex. The multinational firm is affected by the environment and it, in its turn, affects the environment. For instance, in the Politicizing multinational the international rules and regulations applicable to a certain industry can be as much a consequence of the actions of multinational firms as a result of action on the part of governments. In general, the border between what is inside the multinational firm and what is outside becomes quite blurred. In the Networking multinational a subsidiary's close relationship with customers or suppliers may be perceived from an operational point of view to be more internal than the relationships with sister units. Or expressed differently, the difference between the legal border and the operational border can be quite substantial. In the Designing multinational, on the other hand, there is no doubt that the boundary with the environment coincides with the legal border of the multinational firm.

## THEORIES AND ATTITUDES

The differences in basic assumptions and emphasis partly explain the difference in attitudes concerning the multinational firm as a member of society. This is illustrated in the last row in Table 8.1. Some perspectives put the multinational on the 'bright side' more or less by definition, perhaps as a reaction to the negative perspective taken by Hymer in the initial work in this field. The Coordinating multinational is the most obvious example here. The multinational firm is a cost-efficient instrument for coordinating economic transactions across borders, which is also beneficial for society as a whole. The conceptualization of the multinational as a 'social community' in the account of the Knowing multinational has a similar flavour, although based on other arguments. In the Designing multinational the very existence of the multinational firm is proof enough that it is beneficial for society; it exists because it is efficient at adapting to environmental complexities. Implicit to this story is the assumption that competition among firms is strong enough to ensure that only the most efficient ones survive. In the long run there are no harmful monopolies.

The stories above stress the instrumental, functionalistic side of the multinational firm. However, the Dominating multinational also implies an instrumental perspective. The firm is the headquarters' instrument for the exploitation of a firm-specific advantage. But in contrast to the former perspectives, Hymer was under no illusion about the power and interest behind that instrument. Owing to their dominance, multinationals could very easily be detrimental to social welfare. Or, to put it differently, governments have every reason to try to curtail the behaviour of multinationals through legislation because the interests of the multinationals do not automatically coincide with the interests of society.

The Networking and the Politicizing multinationals are neither instruments nor functional entities by definition. Rather, they are primarily complex organizations with a myriad of sub-processes at different levels. The headquarters has less than complete control over these processes and the multinational firm cannot solely be envisaged as an instrument for fulfilling the headquarters' goal. It is, rather, an arena for conflict on which many subunits are acting. However, the multinational firm can mobilize its considerable resources to utilize in line with the firm's own interests, even if these interests are ambiguous and conflicting. The outcome of this mobilization is not as clear and straightforward as in the Dominating multinational – to conquer and dominate global markets – but the problem is similar, arising from the risk of the multinational firm being too large and powerful in society.

In Chapter 1, I claimed that different statements about the societal role of multinational firms reflect underlying assumptions related to these firms as theoretical constructs. These constructs can be more or less explicit, but they are always there, somewhere. If we detect and understand the underlying theories, we can also understand why some statements are on the 'bright side' and some are on the 'dark side'. So, to summarize this chapter I will look back at the quotations made at the beginning of Chapter 1. The quotes from Dunning reflect a view of the multinational firm as a contributor to prosperity through the upgrading of resources in different countries, where the possibility of conflict between society and the multinational firm is downplayed. It is quite obvious that the statements are based on the assumption that multinational firms possess abilities to create values and to transfer these values to new places. This is, in fact, what the entire story of the Knowing multinational is about. The part concerning the harmonious relationships between governments and multinational firms also tells us that neither the Networking multinational nor the Politicizing multinational has been the main inspiration for Dunning in making these statements.

The quotation from Castells also reveals that the multinational firm is predominantly seen as an efficient network for transactions of goods and services across countries. This is essentially what the tales of the Coordinating and Designing multinationals tell us. The first story claims that the multinational is superior at coordinating goods and services within the firm across borders. The second story claims that the multinational is superior in building up an information system for managing this coordination efficiently. If the assumptions behind these stories are questioned, Castells's statement may also be questioned.

On the 'dark side', similar comments can be made. The quotation by van Tulder and van der Zwart reveals a concern for the relative strength of the multinational firm in relation to other producers, and the risk of the multinational firms taking over the local business. This clearly echoes Hymer and his view of market power. If, instead, we were to adopt the view underlying the Coordinating multinational on this issue, the statement in the quotation would become irrelevant.

The quotation from Hertz also echoes Hymer to a great extent. But her statement is even more in line with the Networking and Politicizing multinational owing to her notion of the political power of multinationals and the fact that they are able to 'determine the rules of the game'.

Korten's statement about the large and bureaucratic multinational being a problem is far from the stories recounted of the

Designing multinational and the Coordinating multinational. In the former story, bureaucracy would not be a problem at all because of the efficient design of the multinational in terms of, for example, decentralization. In the latter story, bureaucracy is a prerequisite because it offers the possibility of applying the necessary level of constraint. In contrast, Korten's statement is much easier to relate to the Networking and Politicizing multinational.

Finally, the quotation from Prahalad provides an example of the difficulty of combining conflicting theories. On the one hand, he seems to be convinced that multinationals automatically contribute to social welfare, much in line with the Coordinating and Designing multinational. On the other hand, he claims that they have not tapped into the immense potential for profits in the market of the 4 billion poorest people. Someone, therefore, should tell the firms about this opportunity. Why they have failed to explore this fantastic market, though, is not explained. The conclusion is far from the instrumental and functionalistic views underpinning the Coordinating and Designing multinational, in which competition automatically forces the firm to detect and adapt to changes and opportunities in the environment. On the contrary, the assumed ignorance and inactivity of the multinationals in these markets seem to be more in line with the less instrumental and functionalistic features of some of the other tales in this book.

Prahalad's view offers a good illustration of the importance of making more explicit the underlying premises. This book has hopefully contributed to an increased ability to do so concerning some central theories of the multinational firm.

# Appendix

*Table A.1*    *The world's top 100 non-financial multinational firms, ranked by foreign assets, 2008[a] (millions of dollars and number of employees)*

Ranking by:

| Foreign assets | TNI[b] | Corporation | Home economy | Industry[c] |
|---|---|---|---|---|
| 1 | 75 | General Electric | United States | Electrical & electronic equipment |
| 2 | 32 | Royal Dutch Shell | United Kingdom | Petroleum expl./ref./ distr. |
| 3 | 6 | Vodafone Group Plc | United Kingdom | Telecommunications |
| 4 | 20 | BP PLC | United Kingdom | Petroleum expl./ref./ distr. |
| 5 | 74 | Toyota Motor Corporation | Japan | Motor vehicles |
| 6 | 42 | ExxonMobil Corporation | United States | Petroleum expl./ref./ distr. |
| 7 | 27 | Total SA | France | Petroleum expl./ref./ distr. |
| 8 | 67 | E.ON | Germany | Utilities (electricity, gas and water) |
| 9 | 90 | Electricité de France | France | Utilities (electricity, gas and water) |
| 10 | 10 | ArcelorMittal | Luxembourg | Metal and metal products |
| 11 | 53 | Volkswagen Group | Germany | Motor vehicles |
| 12 | 64 | GDF Suez | France | Utilities (electricity, gas and water) |
| 13 | 8 | Anheuser-Busch Inbev SA | Netherlands | Food, beverages and tobacco |
| 14 | 59 | Chevron Corporation | United States | Petroleum expl./ref./ distr. |
| 15 | 33 | Siemens AG | Germany | Electrical & electronic equipment |
| 16 | 71 | Ford Motor Company | United States | Motor vehicles |
| 17 | 62 | Eni Group | Italy | Petroleum expl./ref./ distr. |
| 18 | 39 | Telefonica SA | Spain | Telecommunications |
| 19 | 79 | Deutsche Telekom AG | Germany | Telecommunications |

| Assets | | Sales | | Employment | | TNI[b] (per cent) |
|---|---|---|---|---|---|---|
| Foreign | Total | Foreign | Total | Foreign[d] | Total | |
| 401 290 | 797 769 | 97 214 | 182 515 | 171 000 | 323 000 | 52.2 |
| 222 324 | 282 401 | 261 393 | 458 361 | 85 000 | 102 000 | 73.0 |
| 201 570 | 218 955 | 60 197 | 69 250 | 68 747 | 79 097 | 88.6 |
| 188 969 | 228 238 | 283 876 | 365 700 | 76 100 | 92 000 | 81.0 |
| 169 569 | 296 249 | 129 724 | 203 955 | 121 755 | 320 808 | 52.9 |
| 161 245 | 228 052 | 321 964 | 459 579 | 50 337 | 79 900 | 67.9 |
| 141 442 | 164 662 | 177 726 | 234 574 | 59 858 | 96 959 | 74.5 |
| 141 168 | 218 573 | 53 020 | 126 925 | 57 134 | 93 538 | 55.8 |
| 133 698 | 278 759 | 43 914 | 94 044 | 51 385 | 160 913 | 42.2 |
| 127 127 | 133 088 | 112 689 | 124 936 | 239 455 | 315 867 | 87.2 |
| 123 677 | 233 708 | 126 007 | 166 508 | 195 586 | 369 928 | 60.5 |
| 119 374 | 232 718 | 68 992 | 99 377 | 95 018 | 196 592 | 56.4 |
| 106 247 | 113 170 | 18 699 | 23 558 | 108 425 | 119 874 | 87.9 |
| 106 129 | 161 165 | 153 854 | 273 005 | 35 000 | 67 000 | 58.1 |
| 104 488 | 135 102 | 84 322 | 116 089 | 295 000 | 427 000 | 73.0 |
| 102 588 | 222 977 | 85 901 | 146 277 | 124 000 | 213 000 | 54.3 |
| 95 818 | 162 269 | 95 448 | 158 227 | 39 400 | 78 880 | 56.4 |
| 95 446 | 139 034 | 54 124 | 84 778 | 197 096 | 251 775 | 70.3 |
| 95 019 | 171 385 | 47 960 | 90 221 | 96 034 | 227 747 | 50.3 |

*Table A.1*    (continued)

| Foreign assets | TNI[b] | Corporation | Home economy | Industry[c] |
|---|---|---|---|---|
| 20 | 37 | Honda Motor Co. Ltd | Japan | Motor vehicles |
| 21 | 70 | Daimler AG | Germany | Motor vehicles |
| 22 | 77 | France Telecom | France | Telecommunications |
| 23 | 88 | ConocoPhillips | United States | Petroleum expl./ref./ distr. |
| 24 | 63 | Iberdrola SA | Spain | Utilities (electricity, gas and water) |
| 25 | 18 | Hutchison Whampoa Limited | Hong Kong, China | Diversified |
| 26 | 36 | EADS NV | France | Aircraft |
| 27 | 11 | Nestlé SA | Switzerland | Food, beverages and tobacco |
| 28 | 78 | BMW AG | Germany | Motor vehicles |
| 29 | 55 | Procter & Gamble | United States | Diversified |
| 30 | 97 | Wal-Mart Stores | United States | Retail & trade |
| 31 | 21 | Roche Group | Switzerland | Pharmaceuticals |
| 32 | 96 | Mitsubishi Corporation | Japan | Wholesale trade |
| 33 | 48 | Sony Corporation | Japan | Electrical & electronic equipment |
| 34 | 56 | Nissan Motor Co. Ltd | Japan | Motor vehicles |
| 35 | 40 | Grupo Ferrovial | Spain | Construction and real estate |
| 36 | 92 | RWE Group | Germany | Utilities (electricity, gas and water) |
| 37 | 1 | Xstrata PLC | United Kingdom | Mining & quarrying |
| 38 | 50 | IBM | United States | Electrical & electronic equipment |
| 39 | 57 | Sanofi-aventis | France | Pharmaceuticals |
| 40 | 3 | Nokia | Finland | Electrical & electronic equipment |
| 41 | 16 | Lafarge SA | France | Non-metallic mineral products |
| 42 | 72 | Pfizer Inc. | United States | Pharmaceuticals |
| 43 | 45 | Mitsui & Co Ltd. | Japan | Wholesale trade |

| Assets | | Sales | | Employment | | TNI[b] (per cent) |
|---|---|---|---|---|---|---|
| Foreign | Total | Foreign | Total | Foreign[d] | Total | |
| 89 204 | 120 478 | 80 861 | 99 458 | 111 581 | 181 876 | 72.2 |
| 87 927 | 184 021 | 108 348 | 140 268 | 105 463 | 273 216 | 54.5 |
| 81 378 | 132 630 | 36 465 | 78 256 | 83 795 | 186 049 | 51.0 |
| 77 864 | 142 865 | 74 346 | 240 842 | 15 128 | 33 800 | 43.4 |
| 73 576 | 119 467 | 19 785 | 36 863 | 17 778 | 32 993 | 56.4 |
| 70 762 | 87 745 | 25 006 | 30 236 | 182 148 | 220 000 | 82.0 |
| 66 950 | 105 989 | 57 890 | 63 299 | 73 969 | 118 349 | 72.4 |
| 66 316 | 99 854 | 99 559 | 101 466 | 274 043 | 283 000 | 87.1 |
| 63 201 | 140 690 | 62 119 | 77 830 | 26 125 | 100 041 | 50.3 |
| 62 942 | 134 833 | 47 949 | 79 029 | 99 019 | 135 000 | 60.2 |
| 62 514 | 163 429 | 98 645 | 401 244 | 648 905 | 2 100 000 | 31.2 |
| 60 927 | 71 532 | 42 114 | 42 590 | 45 510 | 80 080 | 80.3 |
| 59 160 | 111 295 | 6 634 | 61 063 | 18 027 | 60 095 | 31.3 |
| 57 116 | 122 462 | 58 185 | 76 795 | 107 900 | 171 300 | 61.8 |
| 57 080 | 104 379 | 60 693 | 83 819 | 81 249 | 160 422 | 59.2 |
| 54 322 | 67 088 | 13 156 | 20 667 | 64 309 | 106 596 | 68.3 |
| 53 557 | 130 035 | 26 710 | 71 617 | 26 688 | 65 908 | 39.7 |
| 52 227 | 55 314 | 25 215 | 27 952 | 37 883 | 39 940 | 93.2 |
| 52 020 | 109 524 | 66 944 | 103 630 | 283 455 | 398 455 | 61.1 |
| 50 328 | 100 191 | 22 636 | 40 334 | 69 990 | 98 213 | 59.2 |
| 50 006 | 55 090 | 73 662 | 74 192 | 101 559 | 125 829 | 90.3 |
| 50 003 | 56 518 | 23 865 | 27 846 | 65 520 | 83 438 | 84.2 |
| 49 151 | 111 148 | 27 861 | 48 296 | 49 929 | 81 800 | 54.3 |
| 48 653 | 85 262 | 23 299 | 54 991 | 37 810 | 39 864 | 64.8 |

*Table A.1*    (continued)

| Foreign assets | TNI[b] | Corporation | Home economy | Industry[c] |
|---|---|---|---|---|
| 44 | 58 | Hewlett-Packard | United States | Electrical & electronic equipment |
| 45 | 85 | Rio Tinto Plc | United Kingdom | Mining & quarrying |
| 46 | 9 | Anglo American | United Kingdom | Mining & quarrying |
| 47 | 47 | Veolia Environnement SA | France | Utilities (electricity, gas and water) |
| 48 | 100 | CITIC Group | China | Diversified |
| 49 | 35 | Compagnie de Saint-Gobain SA | France | Non-metallic mineral products |
| 50 | 41 | Novartis | Switzerland | Pharmaceuticals |
| 51 | 66 | BASF AG | Germany | Chemicals |
| 52 | 52 | Fiat SpA | Italy | Motor vehicles |
| 53 | 84 | General Motors | United States | Motor vehicles |
| 54 | 76 | Johnson & Johnson | United States | Pharmaceuticals |
| 55 | 19 | Cemex S.A. | Mexico | Non-metallic mineral products |
| 56 | 94 | Statoil ASA | Norway | Petroleum expl./ref./distr. |
| 57 | 17 | Volvo AB | Sweden | Motor vehicles |
| 58 | 14 | AstraZeneca Plc | United Kingdom | Pharmaceuticals |
| 59 | 80 | Vivendi Universal | France | Telecommunications |
| 60 | 61 | BHP Billiton Group | Australia | Mining & quarrying |
| 61 | 13 | Liberty Global Inc. | United States | Telecommunications |
| 62 | 54 | National Grid Transco | United Kingdom | Utilities (electricity, gas and water) |
| 63 | 23 | BAE Systems Plc | United Kingdom | Aircraft |
| 64 | 81 | Repsol YPF SA | Spain | Petroleum expl./ref./distr. |
| 65 | 24 | Philips Electronics | Netherlands | Electrical & electronic equipment |
| 66 | 4 | Pernod Ricard SA | France | Food, beverages and tobacco |
| 67 | 5 | WPP Group Plc | United Kingdom | Business services |
| 68 | 60 | Thyssenkrupp AG | Germany | Metal and metal products |

Ranking by: Foreign assets  TNI[b]  Corporation  Home economy  Industry[c]

| Assets | | Sales | | Employment | | TNI[b] (per cent) |
|---|---|---|---|---|---|---|
| Foreign | Total | Foreign | Total | Foreign[d] | Total | |
| 48 258 | 113 331 | 81 432 | 118 364 | 209 708 | 321 000 | 58.9 |
| 47 064 | 89 616 | 21 649 | 58 065 | 54 156 | 105 785 | 47.0 |
| 44 413 | 49 738 | 21 766 | 26 311 | 95 000 | 105 000 | 87.5 |
| 43 990 | 68 373 | 31 723 | 52 971 | 220 106 | 336 013 | 63.2 |
| 43 750 | 238 725 | 5 427 | 22 230 | 18 305 | 90 650 | 21.0 |
| 43 597 | 60 397 | 45 834 | 64 082 | 153 614 | 209 175 | 72.4 |
| 43 505 | 78 299 | 40 928 | 41 459 | 48 328 | 96 717 | 68.1 |
| 43 020 | 70 786 | 50 925 | 91 154 | 49 560 | 96 924 | 55.9 |
| 40 851 | 85 974 | 65 931 | 86 876 | 115 977 | 198 348 | 60.6 |
| 40 532 | 91 047 | 73 597 | 148 979 | 127 000 | 243 000 | 48.7 |
| 40 324 | 84 912 | 31 438 | 63 747 | 69 700 | 118 700 | 51.8 |
| 40 258 | 45 084 | 17 982 | 21 830 | 41 586 | 56 791 | 81.6 |
| 37 977 | 82 645 | 28 328 | 116 318 | 11 495 | 29 496 | 36.4 |
| 37 582 | 47 472 | 43 946 | 46 047 | 73 190 | 101 380 | 82.3 |
| 36 973 | 46 784 | 29 691 | 31 601 | 54 183 | 65 000 | 85.4 |
| 35 879 | 78 867 | 13 789 | 37 150 | 30 135 | 44 243 | 50.2 |
| 34 393 | 78 770 | 34 784 | 50 211 | 24 730 | 40 990 | 57.8 |
| 33 904 | 33 986 | 10 561 | 10 561 | 13 128 | 22 300 | 86.2 |
| 33 680 | 63 761 | 17 373 | 26 379 | 17 429 | 27 886 | 60.4 |
| 33 285 | 37 427 | 25 249 | 30 583 | 61 200 | 94 000 | 78.9 |
| 32 720 | 68 795 | 43 970 | 84 477 | 18 403 | 36 302 | 50.1 |
| 32 675 | 45 986 | 37 122 | 38 603 | 83 946 | 121 398 | 78.8 |
| 32 237 | 35 159 | 8 845 | 9 850 | 16 260 | 18 975 | 89.1 |
| 31 567 | 35 661 | 11 966 | 13 717 | 88 467 | 97 438 | 88.9 |
| 31 422 | 59 557 | 51 441 | 80 207 | 114 277 | 199 374 | 58.1 |

*Table A.1*    (continued)

| Ranking by: | | | | |
|---|---|---|---|---|
| Foreign assets | TNI[b] | Corporation | Home economy | Industry[c] |
| 69 | 46 | Vattenfall | Sweden | Electricity, gas and water |
| 70 | 86 | Deutsche Post AG | Germany | Transport and storage |
| 71 | 38 | Unilever | United Kingdom | Diversified |
| 72 | 7 | Linde AG | Germany | Chemicals |
| 73 | 26 | BG Group Plc | United Kingdom | Electricity, gas and water |
| 74 | 43 | Pinault-Printemps Redoute SA | France | Retail & trade |
| 75 | 34 | TeliaSonera AB | Sweden | Telecommunications |
| 76 | 73 | Samsung Electronics Co., Ltd | Korea, Republic of | Electrical & electronic equipment |
| 77 | 51 | Metro AG | Germany | Retail & trade |
| 78 | 99 | Petronas - Petroliam Nasional Bhd | Malaysia | Petroleum expl./ref./ distr. |
| 79 | 93 | Hyundai Motor Company | Korea, Republic of | Motor vehicles |
| 80 | 83 | China Ocean Shipping (Group) Company | China | Transport and storage |
| 81 | 65 | Carrefour SA | France | Retail & trade |
| 82 | 22 | CRH Plc | Ireland | Non-metallic mineral products |
| 83 | 44 | Holcim AG | Switzerland | Non-metallic mineral products |
| 84 | 89 | EDP Energias de Portugal SA | Portugal | Utilities (electricity, gas and water) |
| 85 | 49 | Alcoa | United States | Metal and metal products |
| 86 | 68 | GlaxoSmithKline Plc | United Kingdom | Pharmaceuticals |
| 87 | 2 | ABB Ltd | Switzerland | Engineering services |
| 88 | 12 | Air Liquide | France | Chemical/non-metallic mineral products |
| 89 | 69 | United Technologies Corporation | United States | Aircraft |

| Assets | | Sales | | Employment | | TNI[b] (per cent) |
|---|---|---|---|---|---|---|
| Foreign | Total | Foreign | Total | Foreign[d] | Total | |
| 31 288 | 56 829 | 16 079 | 24 952 | 23 675 | 32 801 | 63.9 |
| 30 765 | 365 990 | 55 170 | 79 699 | 283 699 | 451 515 | 46.8 |
| 30 236 | 50 302 | 40 483 | 59 287 | 144 000 | 174 000 | 70.4 |
| 29 847 | 33 158 | 16 574 | 18 527 | 44 278 | 51 908 | 88.3 |
| 29 832 | 36 437 | 18 239 | 23 053 | 3 639 | 5 395 | 76.1 |
| 29 362 | 37 617 | 18 056 | 29 555 | 55 169 | 88 025 | 67.3 |
| 29 067 | 33 688 | 10 265 | 15 707 | 19 885 | 30 037 | 72.6 |
| 28 765 | 83 738 | 88 892 | 110 321 | 77 236 | 161 700 | 54.2 |
| 28 729 | 47 077 | 60 410 | 99 424 | 161 925 | 265 974 | 60.9 |
| 28 447 | 106 416 | 32 477 | 77 094 | 7 847 | 39 236 | 29.6 |
| 28 359 | 82 072 | 33 874 | 72 523 | 22 066 | 78 270 | 36.5 |
| 28 066 | 36 253 | 18 041 | 27 431 | 4 581 | 69 648 | 49.9 |
| 28 056 | 72 487 | 71 688 | 127 238 | 363 311 | 495 287 | 56.1 |
| 27 787 | 29 396 | 28 926 | 30 559 | 46 248 | 93 572 | 79.5 |
| 27 312 | 42 487 | 14 323 | 23 225 | 63 156 | 86 713 | 66.3 |
| 27 104 | 49 699 | 7 679 | 20 328 | 4 543 | 12 245 | 43.1 |
| 26 973 | 37 822 | 12 566 | 26 901 | 57 000 | 87 000 | 61.2 |
| 26 924 | 57 424 | 28 030 | 44 674 | 54 326 | 99 003 | 54.8 |
| 26 875 | 33 181 | 33 166 | 34 912 | 113 900 | 119 600 | 90.4 |
| 26 647 | 28 678 | 15 292 | 19 170 | 37 876 | 43 000 | 86.9 |
| 26 451 | 56 469 | 30 729 | 58 681 | 145 015 | 223 100 | 54.7 |

*Table A.1*    (continued)

| Ranking by: | | | | |
| Foreign assets | TNI[b] | Corporation | Home economy | Industry[c] |
| --- | --- | --- | --- | --- |
| 90 | 91 | Sumitomo Corporation | Japan | Wholesale trade |
| 91 | 30 | LMVH Moët-Hennessy Louis Vuitton SA | France | Other consumer goods |
| 92 | 87 | Bayer AG | Germany | Pharmaceuticals |
| 93 | 82 | Kraft Foods Inc. | United States | Food, beverages and tobacco |
| 94 | 28 | SAB Miller | United Kingdom | Food, beverages and tobacco |
| 95 | 29 | Coca-Cola Company | United States | Food, beverages and tobacco |
| 96 | 95 | Marubeni Corporation | Japan | Wholesale trade |
| 97 | 25 | Schlumberger Ltd | United States | Other consumer services |
| 98 | 98 | Hitachi Ltd | Japan | Electrical & electronic equipment |
| 99 | 31 | Diageo Plc | United Kingdom | Food, beverages and tobacco |
| 100 | 15 | Teva Pharmaceutical Industries Limited | Israel | Pharmaceuticals |

*Notes:*
[a] All data are based on the companies' annual reports unless otherwise stated.
[b] TNI, the Transnationlity Index, is calculated as the average of the following three ratios: foreign assets to total assets, foreign sales to total sales and foreign employment to total employment.
[c] Industry classification for companies follows the United States Standard Industrial Classification as used by the United States Securities and Exchange Commission (SEC).
[d] In a number of cases foreign employment data were calculated by applying the share of foreign employment in total employment of the previous year to total employment of 2008.

*Source:*    UNCTAD/Erasmus University database.

| Assets | | Sales | | Employment | | TNI[b] (per cent) |
|---|---|---|---|---|---|---|
| Foreign | Total | Foreign | Total | Foreign[d] | Total | |
| 26 448 | 70 890 | 18 238 | 35 470 | 26 397 | 70 755 | 42.0 |
| 26 377 | 43 949 | 21 549 | 25 154 | 57 350 | 77 087 | 73.4 |
| 25 696 | 73 084 | 24 979 | 48 161 | 53 100 | 108 600 | 45.3 |
| 25 638 | 63 078 | 20 765 | 42 201 | 59 000 | 98 000 | 50.0 |
| 25 139 | 31 619 | 12 585 | 18 703 | 52 362 | 68 635 | 74.4 |
| 25 136 | 40 519 | 23 930 | 31 944 | 79 400 | 92 400 | 74.3 |
| 25 049 | 47 985 | 13 824 | 39 762 | 653 | 3 856 | 34.6 |
| 24 821 | 31 991 | 20 483 | 27 163 | 67 502 | 87 000 | 76.9 |
| 24 282 | 95 858 | 32 956 | 99 350 | 127 277 | 361 796 | 31.2 |
| 24 264 | 29 965 | 17 086 | 19 603 | 12 379 | 24 270 | 73.0 |
| 24 213 | 32 904 | 10 609 | 11 085 | 32 146 | 38 307 | 84.4 |

*Table A.2*   *The top 100 non-financial multinationals from developing*
*and transition economies, ranked by foreign assets, 2008[a]*
*(millions of dollars and number of employees)*

Ranking by:

| Foreign assets | TNI[b] | Corporation | Home economy | Industry[c] |
|---|---|---|---|---|
| 1 | 9 | Hutchison Whampoa Limited | Hong Kong, China | Diversified |
| 2 | 88 | CITIC Group | China | Diversified |
| 3 | 11 | Cemex S.A. | Mexico | Non-metallic mineral products |
| 4 | 41 | Samsung Electronics Co., Ltd | Korea, Republic of | Electrical & electronic equipment |
| 5 | 79 | Petronas – Petroliam Nasional Bhd | Malaysia | Petroleum expl./ref./ distr. |
| 6 | 71 | Hyundai Motor Company | Korea, Republic of | Motor vehicles |
| 7 | 46 | China Ocean Shipping (Group) Company | China | Transport and storage |
| 8 | 61 | Lukoil | Russian Federation | Petroleum and natural gas |
| 9 | 67 | Vale S.A. | Brazil | Mining & quarrying |
| 10 | 85 | Petróleos de Venezuela | Venezuela, Bolivarian Republic of | Petroleum expl./ref./ distr. |
| 11 | 30 | Zain | Kuwait | Telecommunications |
| 12 | 22 | Jardine Matheson Holdings Ltd | Hong Kong, China | Diversified |
| 13 | 29 | Singtel Ltd | Singapore | Telecommunications |
| 14 | 64 | Formosa Plastics Group | Taiwan Province of China | Chemicals |
| 15 | 18 | Tata Steel Ltd | India | Metal and metal products |
| 16 | 91 | Petroleo Brasileiro S.A. - Petrobras | Brazil | Petroleum expl./ref./ distr. |
| 17 | 35 | Hon Hai Precision Industries | Taiwan Province of China | Electrical & electronic equipment |
| 18 | 49 | Metalurgica Gerdau S.A. | Brazil | Metal and metal products |

| Assets | | Sales | | Employment | | TNI[b] (per cent) |
|---|---|---|---|---|---|---|
| Foreign | Total | Foreign | Total | Foreign[d] | Total | |
| 70762 | 87745 | 25006 | 30236 | 182148 | 220000 | 82.0 |
| 43750 | 238725 | 5427 | 22230 | 18305 | 90650 | 21.0 |
| 40258 | 45084 | 17982 | 21830 | 41586 | 56791 | 81.6 |
| 28765 | 83738 | 88892 | 110321 | 77236 | 161700 | 54.2 |
| 28447 | 106416 | 32477 | 77094 | 7847 | 39236 | 29.6 |
| 28359 | 82072 | 33874 | 72523 | 22066 | 78270 | 36.5 |
| 28066 | 36253 | 18041 | 27431 | 4581 | 69648 | 49.9 |
| 21515 | 71461 | 87637 | 107680 | 23000 | 152500 | 42.2 |
| 19635 | 79931 | 30939 | 37426 | 4725 | 62490 | 38.3 |
| 19244 | 131832 | 52494 | 126364 | 5140 | 61909 | 21.5 |
| 18746 | 19761 | 6034 | 7452 | 1151 | 15000 | 61.2 |
| 17544 | 22098 | 16831 | 22362 | 79276 | 150000 | 69.2 |
| 17326 | 21887 | 6745 | 10374 | 9058 | 20000 | 63.2 |
| 16937 | 76587 | 17078 | 66259 | 70519 | 94268 | 40.9 |
| 16826 | 23868 | 26426 | 32168 | 45864 | 80782 | 69.8 |
| 15075 | 125695 | 40179 | 146529 | 6775 | 74240 | 16.2 |
| 14664 | 26771 | 21727 | 61810 | 515626 | 611000 | 58.1 |
| 13658 | 25750 | 10274 | 23182 | 22315 | 46000 | 48.6 |

*Table A.2*   (continued)

| Foreign assets | TNI[b] | Corporation | Home economy | Industry[c] |
|---|---|---|---|---|
| 19 | 21 | Abu Dhabi National Energy Company | United Arab Emirates | Utilities (electricity, gas and water) |
| 20 | 82 | Oil and Natural Gas Corporation | India | Petroleum expl./ref./ distr. |
| 21 | 24 | MTN Group Limited | South Africa | Telecommunications |
| 22 | 58 | LG Corp. | Korea, Republic of | Electrical & electronic equipment |
| 23 | 53 | Evraz | Russian Federation | Metal and metal products |
| 24 | 20 | Qatar Telecom | Qatar | Telecommunications |
| 25 | 44 | América Móvil | Mexico | Telecommunications |
| 26 | 33 | Capitaland Limited | Singapore | Construction and real estate |
| 27 | 100 | China National Petroleum Corporation | China | Petroleum expl./ref./ distr. |
| 28 | 69 | New World Development Co., Ltd | Hong Kong, China | Diversified |
| 29 | 17 | Hindalco Industries Limited | India | Diversified |
| 30 | 74 | STX Corporation | Korea, Republic of | Other equipment |
| 31 | 23 | Axiata Group Bhd | Malaysia | Telecommunications |
| 32 | 77 | Severstal | Russian Federation | Metal and metal products |
| 33 | 34 | Wilmar International Limited | Singapore | Food, beverages and tobacco |
| 34 | 7 | China Resources Enterprises | Hong Kong, China | Petroleum expl./ref./ distr. |
| 35 | 2 | China Merchants Holdings International | Hong Kong, China | Diversified |
| 36 | 27 | Ternium SA | Argentina | Metal and metal products |

| Assets | | Sales | | Employment | | TNI[b] (per cent) |
|---|---|---|---|---|---|---|
| Foreign | Total | Foreign | Total | Foreign[d] | Total | |
| 13 519 | 23 523 | 3 376 | 4 576 | 1 839 | 2 383 | 69.5 |
| 13 477 | 30 456 | 4 238 | 27 684 | 3 921 | 33 035 | 23.8 |
| 13 266 | 18 281 | 7 868 | 12 403 | 10 870 | 16 452 | 67.4 |
| 13 256 | 51 517 | 44 439 | 82 060 | 32 962 | 64 000 | 43.8 |
| 11 196 | 19 448 | 12 805 | 20 380 | 29 480 | 134 000 | 47.5 |
| 10 598 | 20 412 | 4 077 | 5 582 | 1 539 | 1 832 | 69.7 |
| 10 428 | 31 481 | 17 323 | 31 026 | 36 353 | 52 879 | 52.6 |
| 9 852 | 17 429 | 1 355 | 1 946 | 5 935 | 10 500 | 60.9 |
| 9 409 | 264 016 | 4 384 | 165 224 | 20 489 | 1 086 966 | 2.7 |
| 9 061 | 22 775 | 1 304 | 3 144 | 17 262 | 55 000 | 37.5 |
| 8 564 | 12 653 | 11 371 | 14 338 | 13 447 | 19 867 | 71.6 |
| 8 308 | 18 338 | 1 668 | 12 914 | 246 | 544 | 34.5 |
| 8 184 | 10 783 | 1 746 | 3 406 | 18 975 | 25 000 | 67.7 |
| 8 066 | 22 480 | 9 325 | 22 393 | 12 662 | 96 695 | 30.2 |
| 7 812 | 17 869 | 22 144 | 29 145 | 12 906 | 23 313 | 58.4 |
| 7 371 | 9 013 | 7 483 | 8 299 | 136 800 | 144 000 | 89.0 |
| 7 154 | 7 388 | 564 | 595 | 4 988 | 5 055 | 96.8 |
| 7 063 | 10 671 | 5 357 | 8 465 | 10 042 | 15 651 | 64.5 |

*Table A.2*    (continued)

| Foreign assets | TNI[b] | Corporation | Home economy | Industry[c] |
|---|---|---|---|---|
| 37 | 90 | China State Construction Engineering Corp. | China | Construction and real estate |
| 38 | 51 | YTL Corp. Berhad | Malaysia | Utilities (electricity, gas and water) |
| 39 | 1 | First Pacific Company Limited | Hong Kong, China | Electrical & electronic equipment |
| 40 | 48 | Tata Motors Ltd | India | Automobile |
| 41 | 38 | Asustek Computer Inc. | Taiwan Province of China | Electrical & electronic equipment |
| 42 | 28 | Orascom Telecom Holding | Egypt | Telecommunications |
| 43 | 62 | Quanta Computer Inc. | Taiwan Province of China | Electrical & electronic equipment |
| 44 | 78 | Sasol Limited | South Africa | Chemicals |
| 45 | 32 | Shangri-La Asia Limited | Hong Kong, China | Other consumer services |
| 46 | 25 | Orient Overseas International Ltd | Hong Kong, China | Transport and storage |
| 47 | 70 | Sinochem Corp. | China | Petroleum expl./ref./distr. |
| 48 | 72 | CLP Holdings | Hong Kong, China | Utilities (electricity, gas and water) |
| 49 | 8 | Sappi Limited | South Africa | Wood and paper products |
| 50 | 89 | JSFC Sistema | Russian Federation | Telecommunications |
| 51 | 37 | Netcare Limited | South Africa | Other consumer services |
| 52 | 26 | Flextronics International Ltd | Singapore | Electrical & electronic equipment |
| 53 | 86 | Posco | Korea, Republic of | Metal and metal products |
| 54 | 15 | Suzlon Energy Limited | India | Diversified |
| 55 | 98 | China National Offshore Oil Corp. | China | Petroleum expl./ref./distr. |
| 56 | 50 | Genting Berhad | Malaysia | Other consumer services |

Ranking by:

| Assets | | Sales | | Employment | | TNI[b] (per cent) |
|---|---|---|---|---|---|---|
| Foreign | Total | Foreign | Total | Foreign[d] | Total | |
| 7015 | 29873 | 3619 | 29080 | 15765 | 113251 | 16.6 |
| 7014 | 11102 | 968 | 1966 | 1931 | 6232 | 47.8 |
| 6998 | 7199 | 4105 | 4105 | 66416 | 66452 | 99.0 |
| 6767 | 14359 | 9869 | 15635 | 17998 | 49473 | 48.9 |
| 6746 | 10998 | 9522 | 21157 | 63974 | 104294 | 55.9 |
| 6718 | 9757 | 2947 | 5305 | 11376 | 16522 | 64.4 |
| 6711 | 9250 | 4930 | 25946 | 20297 | 60900 | 41.6 |
| 6679 | 18977 | 7781 | 21676 | 6041 | 34000 | 29.6 |
| 6587 | 6923 | 1120 | 1353 | 1274 | 25100 | 61.0 |
| 6412 | 7702 | 2196 | 6545 | 7012 | 8236 | 67.3 |
| 6409 | 19825 | 34218 | 44280 | 225 | 26632 | 36.8 |
| 6071 | 17138 | 3060 | 6972 | 1589 | 5717 | 35.7 |
| 5933 | 6109 | 5483 | 5863 | 9850 | 15156 | 85.2 |
| 5698 | 29159 | 3983 | 16671 | 11000 | 80000 | 19.1 |
| 5590 | 6642 | 1516 | 2904 | 9203 | 28884 | 56.1 |
| 5338 | 11317 | 15728 | 30948 | 156273 | 160000 | 65.2 |
| 5335 | 37345 | 13512 | 37966 | 2386 | 16707 | 21.4 |
| 5310 | 7370 | 4714 | 5685 | 10087 | 14000 | 75.7 |
| 5247 | 59917 | 4475 | 28028 | 1739 | 51000 | 9.4 |
| 5139 | 8790 | 667 | 2726 | 16631 | 27296 | 47.9 |

*Table A.2*    (continued)

| Foreign assets | TNI[b] | Corporation | Home economy | Industry[c] |
|---|---|---|---|---|
| | Ranking by: | | | |
| 57 | 36 | Steinhoff International Holdings | South Africa | Other consumer goods |
| 58 | 73 | Gold Fields Limited | South Africa | Metal and metal products |
| 59 | 13 | Medi Clinic Corp. Limited | South Africa | Other consumer services |
| 60 | 5 | Li & Fung Limited | Hong Kong, China | Wholesale trade |
| 61 | 40 | Fraser & Neave Limited | Singapore | Food, beverages and tobacco |
| 62 | 16 | Pou Chen Corp. | Taiwan Province of China | Other consumer goods |
| 63 | 12 | Acer Inc. | Taiwan Province of China | Electrical & electronic equipment |
| 64 | 93 | MMC Norilsk Nickel | Russian Federation | Metal and metal products |
| 65 | 60 | Noble Group Limited | Hong Kong, China | Wholesale trade |
| 66 | 55 | Sime Darby Berhad | Malaysia | Diversified |
| 67 | 94 | China Communications Construction Co. | China | Construction and real estate |
| 68 | 80 | Telefonos de Mexico S.A. de C.V. | Mexico | Telecommunications |
| 69 | 68 | Swire Pacific Limited | Hong Kong, China | Business services |
| 70 | 39 | Naspers Limited | South Africa | Other consumer services |
| 71 | 66 | Keppel Corporation Limited | Singapore | Diversified |
| 72 | 75 | Taiwan Semiconductor Manufacturing Co. Ltd | Taiwan Province of China | Electrical & electronic equipment |
| 73 | 3 | Guangdong Investment Limited | Hong Kong, China | Diversified |

| Assets | | Sales | | Employment | | TNI[b] (per cent) |
|---|---|---|---|---|---|---|
| Foreign | Total | Foreign | Total | Foreign[d] | Total | |
| 5 060 | 7 194 | 3 492 | 5 636 | 15 397 | 41 493 | 56.5 |
| 4 839 | 8 491 | 1 443 | 3 223 | 2 594 | 49 715 | 35.7 |
| 4 788 | 5 395 | 1 341 | 2 294 | 15 799 | 17 800 | 78.7 |
| 4 761 | 4 839 | 13 873 | 14 218 | 10 839 | 14 438 | 90.3 |
| 4 717 | 9 444 | 2 222 | 3 519 | 7 724 | 15 134 | 54.7 |
| 4 553 | 6 929 | 5 518 | 6 622 | 226 782 | 345 185 | 71.6 |
| 4 455 | 7 418 | 16 495 | 17 311 | 5 677 | 6 727 | 79.9 |
| 4 389 | 20 823 | 1 998 | 13 980 | 4 000 | 88 100 | 13.3 |
| 4 346 | 8 153 | 11 404 | 36 090 | 2 006 | 4 800 | 42.2 |
| 4 307 | 10 061 | 6 065 | 8 827 | 25 432 | 100 000 | 45.7 |
| 4 010 | 31 911 | 5 599 | 25 740 | 1 703 | 93 019 | 12.1 |
| 3 948 | 13 528 | 2 464 | 11 140 | 18 812 | 54 317 | 28.6 |
| 3 903 | 25 552 | 1 879 | 3 168 | 27 000 | 70 000 | 37.7 |
| 3 821 | 5 746 | 995 | 3 018 | 7 790 | 11 715 | 55.3 |
| 3 820 | 11 636 | 2 562 | 8 346 | 18 352 | 35 621 | 38.3 |
| 3 813 | 17 030 | 6 139 | 10 558 | 2 708 | 22 843 | 30.8 |
| 3 749 | 4 031 | 946 | 975 | 4 063 | 4 267 | 95.1 |

*Table A.2*    (continued)

| Foreign assets | TNI[b] | Corporation | Home economy | Industry[c] |
|---|---|---|---|---|
| 74 | 83 | VimpelCom | Russian Federation | Telecommunications |
| 75 | 14 | Beijing Enterprises Holdings Ltd | China | Diversified |
| 76 | 54 | Enka Insaat ve Sanayi | Turkey | Construction and real estate |
| 77 | 76 | FEMSA-Fomento Economico Mexicano | Mexico | Food, beverages and tobacco |
| 78 | 99 | China Railway Construction Corporation Ltd | China | Construction |
| 79 | 56 | ZTE Corp. | China | Other consumer goods |
| 80 | 95 | Chi MEI Optoelectronics | Taiwan Province of China | Electrical & electronic equipment |
| 81 | 92 | Mechel | Russian Federation | Metal and metal products |
| 82 | 43 | United Microelectronics Corporation | Taiwan Province of China | Electrical & electronic equipment |
| 83 | 31 | Inventec Company | Taiwan Province of China | Electrical & electronic equipment |
| 84 | 63 | Lenovo Group | China | Electrical & electronic equipment |
| 85 | 84 | San Miguel Corporation | Philippines | Food, beverages and tobacco |
| 86 | 45 | Neptune Orient Lines Ltd | Singapore | Transport and storage |
| 87 | 6 | Shougang Concord International | Hong Kong, China | Metal and metal products |
| 88 | 57 | Compal Electronics Inc. | Taiwan Province of China | Other consumer goods |
| 89 | 97 | PTT Public Company Limited | Thailand | Petroleum expl./ref./distr. |
| 90 | 52 | National Industries Group Holdings SAK | Kuwait | Diversified |

Ranking by:

| Assets | | Sales | | Employment | | TNI[b] (per cent) |
|---|---|---|---|---|---|---|
| Foreign | Total | Foreign | Total | Foreign[d] | Total | |
| 3 726 | 15 725 | 1 520 | 10 117 | 10 233 | 38 403 | 21.8 |
| 3 662 | 6 670 | 2 524 | 2 530 | 28 260 | 37 000 | 77.0 |
| 3 540 | 7 767 | 3 256 | 6 956 | 19 286 | 40 886 | 46.5 |
| 3 508 | 13 377 | 4 792 | 15 082 | 40 631 | 122 981 | 30.3 |
| 3 146 | 32 204 | 2 475 | 31 571 | 18 613 | 190 545 | 9.1 |
| 3 143 | 7 642 | 3 860 | 6 373 | 19 031 | 61 350 | 44.2 |
| 3 070 | 18 099 | 187 | 10 081 | 6 325 | 37 623 | 11.9 |
| 2 911 | 12 010 | 1 385 | 9 951 | 8 244 | 83 670 | 16.0 |
| 2 901 | 6 594 | 2 153 | 3 068 | 5 481 | 12 458 | 52.7 |
| 2 874 | 3 935 | 1 911 | 12 016 | 26 294 | 27 799 | 61.2 |
| 2 732 | 6 308 | 8 467 | 14 901 | 5 201 | 22 511 | 41.1 |
| 2 655 | 7 117 | 458 | 3 774 | 2 383 | 15 344 | 21.7 |
| 2 640 | 5 445 | 7 150 | 9 285 | 3 452 | 11 000 | 52.3 |
| 2 630 | 2 713 | 1 783 | 2 243 | 3 546 | 3 900 | 89.1 |
| 2 573 | 5 954 | 4 579 | 15 171 | 25 239 | 43 182 | 43.9 |
| 2 525 | 25 252 | 5 993 | 59 931 | 798 | 7 989 | 10.0 |
| 2 504 | 6 279 | 264 | 420 | 1 364 | 3 423 | 47.5 |

*Table A.2*    (continued)

| Foreign assets | TNI[b] | Corporation | Home economy | Industry[c] |
|---|---|---|---|---|
| 91 | 47 | Tanjong Public Limited Company | Malaysia | Pharmaceuticals |
| 92 | 42 | Qisda Corp. (Benq) | Taiwan Province of China | Electrical & electronic equipment |
| 93 | 4 | Road King Infrastructure Limited | Hong Kong, China | Transport and storage |
| 94 | 81 | TMK | Russian Federation | Metal and metal products |
| 95 | 10 | Techtronic Industries Company Limited | Hong Kong, China | Other equipment |
| 96 | 59 | Wistron Corp. | Taiwan Province of China | Other equipment |
| 97 | 96 | China Minmetals Corp. | China | Metal and metal products |
| 98 | 19 | TPV Technology Limited | China | Wholesale trade |
| 99 | 65 | Agility Public Warehousing Company | Kuwait | Construction and real estate |
| 100 | 87 | Turkcell Iletisim Hizmetleri AS | Turkey | Telecommunications |

Ranking by appears as a heading above Foreign assets and TNI.

*Notes:*
[a] All data are based on the companies' annual reports unless otherwise stated.
[b] TNI, the Transnationality Index, is calculated as the average of the following three ratios: foreign assets to total assets, foreign sales to total sales and foreign employment to total employment.
[c] Industry classification for companies follows the United States Standard Industrial Classification as used by the United States Securities and Exchange Commission (SEC).
[d] In a number of cases foreign employment data were calculated by applying the share of foreign employment in total employment of the previous year to total employment of 2008.

*Source:*    UNCTAD/Erasmus University database.

| Assets | | Sales | | Employment | | TNI[b] (per cent) |
|---|---|---|---|---|---|---|
| Foreign | Total | Foreign | Total | Foreign[d] | Total | |
| 2 445 | 3 451 | 455 | 1 101 | 902 | 2 484 | 49.5 |
| 2 441 | 3 936 | 2 678 | 5 372 | 16 338 | 33 504 | 53.5 |
| 2 428 | 2 698 | 535 | 595 | 1 008 | 1 105 | 90.4 |
| 2 361 | 7 071 | 2 302 | 5 690 | 4 101 | 48 494 | 27.4 |
| 2 334 | 2 811 | 3 418 | 3 418 | 12 098 | 19 354 | 81.8 |
| 2 316 | 4 249 | 2 458 | 14 153 | 20 136 | 35 875 | 42.7 |
| 2 269 | 13 484 | 4 318 | 26 668 | 798 | 44 425 | 11.6 |
| 2 266 | 3 354 | 6 860 | 9 247 | 19 256 | 28 500 | 69.8 |
| 2 264 | 5 949 | 2 719 | 6 845 | 14 242 | 37 418 | 38.6 |
| 2 263 | 8 068 | 514 | 6 970 | 2 979 | 10 620 | 21.2 |

# References

Aldrich, H.E. (1979). *Organizations and Environment*. Englewood Cliffs, NJ: Prentice Hall.

Aliber, R.Z. (1970). A theory of foreign direct investment. In Kindleberger, C.P. (ed.), *The International Corporation*. Cambridge, MA: MIT Press.

Bain, J.S. (1956). *Barriers to New Competition: Their Character and Consequences in Manufacturing Industries*. Cambridge, MA: Harvard University Press.

Barney, J.B. (1991). Firm resources and sustained competitive advantage. *Journal of Management*, **17**, 99–120.

Bartlett, C.A., Ghoshal, S. (1989). *Managing Across Borders: The Transnational Solution*. Cambridge, MA: Harvard Business School Press.

Blumentritt, T.P., Nigh, D. (2002). The integration of subsidiary political activities in multinational corporations. *Journal of International Business Studies*, **33**(1), 57–77.

Buckley, P. (2006). Stephen Hymer: three phases, one approach? *International Business Review*, **15**(2), 140–147.

Buckley, P. (2010). The role of headquarters in the global factory. In Andersson, U., Holm, U. (eds), *Managing the Contemporary Multinational*. Cheltenham, UK and Northampton, MA, USA: Edward Elgar.

Buckley, P., Casson, M. (1991). *The Future of the Multinational Enterprise*. 2nd edition. London: Macmillan.

Buckley, P., Davies, H. (1979). The place of licensing in the theory and practise of foreign operations. University of Reading Discussion Papers in International Investment and Business Studies No. 47.

Buckley, P., Ghauri, P. (2004). Globalization, economic geography and the strategy of multinational enterprises. *Journal of International Business Studies*, **5**(2), 81–97.

Cantwell, J. (1989). *Technological Innovation and Multinational Corporations*. Oxford: Blackwell.

Cantwell, J. (1991). A survey of theories of international production. In Pitelis, C., Sugden, R. (eds), *The Nature of the Transnational Firm*. London: Routledge.

Cantwell, J. (1994). The relationship between international trade and international production. In Greenway, D., Winters, L.A. (eds), *Surveys in International Trade*. Oxford: Blackwell.

Cantwell, J., Mudambi, R. (2005). MNE competence-creating subsidiary mandates. *Strategic Management Journal*, **26**, 1109–1128.

Cantwell, J., Narula, R. (2001). The eclectic paradigm in the global economy. *International Journal of the Economics of Business*, **8**(2), 155–172.

Cantwell, J., Piscitello, L. (2000). Accumulating technological competence: its changing impact on corporate diversification and internationalization. *Industrial and Corporate Change*, **9**(1), 21–51.

Cantwell, J., Santangelo, G. (2000). Capitalism, innovation and profits in the new technoeconomic paradigm. *Journal of Evolutionary Economics*, **10**(1–2), 131–157.

Castells, M. (1996). *The Rise of the Network Society*. Oxford: Blackwell Publishers.

Caves, R.E. (1982). *Multinational Enterprise and Economic Analysis*. Cambridge: Cambridge University Press.

Caves, R.E. (1996). *Multinational Enterprise and Economic Analysis*. 2nd edition. Cambridge: Cambridge University Press.

Chandler, A.D. (1962). *Strategy and Structure: Chapters in the History of Industrial Enterprise*. Cambridge, MA: MIT Press.

Cohen, R.B., Felton, N., van Liere, J., Nkosi, M. (1979). *The Multinational Corporation: A Radical Approach. Papers by Stephen Herbert Hymer*. Cambridge: Cambridge University Press.

Conner, K.R., Prahalad, C.K. (1996). A resource-based view of the firm: knowledge versus opportunism. *Organization Science*, **7**(5), 477–501.

Cyert, R.M., March, J.G. (1963). *A Behavioral Theory of the Firm*. Englewood Cliffs, NJ: Prentice Hall.

DiMaggio, P.J., Powell, W.W. (1983). The iron cage revisited: institutional isomorphism and collective rationality in organizational fields. *American Sociological Review*, **48**, 147–160.

Doane, D. (2005). The myth of CSR. *Stanford Social Innovation Review*, Fall, 23–29.

Dunning, J. (1958). *American Investment in British Manufacturing Industry*. London: George Allen & Unwin.

Dunning, J. (1988). The eclectic paradigm of international production - an update and some possible extensions. *Journal of International Business Studies*, **19**, 1–31.

Dunning, J. (1993). *The Globalization of Business*. London: Routledge.

Dunning, J. (1994). Re-evaluating the benefits of foreign direct investment. *Transnational Corporations*, **3**(1), 23–51.

Dunning, J. (1997). *Alliance Capitalism and Global Business*. London: Routledge.

Eden, L., Lenway, S. (2001). Introduction to the Symposium. Multinationals: the Janus face of globalization. *Journal of International Business Studies*, **32**(3), 383–400.

Edman, J. (2009). *The Paradox of Foreignness*. Stockholm: Institute of International Business, Stockholm School of Business.

Egelhoff, W. (1988). *Organizing the Multinational Enterprise. An Information Processing View*. Cambridge, MA: Ballinger Publishing Company.

Egelhoff, W. (1993). Information processing theory and the multinational corporation. In Ghoshal, S., Westney, E. (eds), *Organization Theory and the Multinational Corporation*. New York: St Martin's Press.

Engwall, L. (2006). Global enterprises in the fields of governance. In Djelic, M.-L., Sahlin-Andersson, K. (eds), *Transnational Governance: Institutional Dynamics of Regulation*. Cambridge: Cambridge University Press.

Erramilli, K.M., Agarwal, S., Dev, C.S. (2002). Choice between non-equity modes: an organizational capability perspective. *Journal of International Business Studies*, **33**(2), 223–242.

Ferner, A., Almond, P., Colling, T. (2005). Institutional theory and the cross-border transfer of employment policy. *Journal of International Business Studies*, **36**(3), 304–321.

Forsgren, M. (2002). Are multinational firms good or bad? In Havila, V., Forsgren, M., Håkansson, H. (eds), *Critical Perspectives on Internationalization*. Amsterdam: Pergamon.

Forsgren, M. (2008). Are multinationals superior or just powerful? A critical review of the evolutionary theory of the MNC. In Dunning, J., Gugler, P. (eds), *Foreign Direct Investment, Location and Competitiveness*. Amsterdam: Elsevier.

Forsgren, M., Johanson, J. (1992). Managing internationalization in business networks. In Forsgren, M., Johanson, J. (eds), *Managing Networks in International Business*. Philadelphia, PA: Gordon & Breach.

Forsgren, M., Holm, U., Johanson, J. (2005). *Managing the Embedded Multinational. A Business Network View*. Cheltenham, UK and Northampton, MA, USA: Edward Elgar.

Foss, N.J. (1997). On the rationales of corporate headquarters. *Industrial and Corporate Change*, **6**(2), 313–338.

Frank, R.H., Freeman, R.T. (1978). *Distributed Consequences of Direct Foreign Investment*. New York: Academic Press.

Franko, L.G. (1976). *The European Multinationals: A Renewed Challenge to American and British Big Business*. Stamford, CT: Greylock Publishing.

Gebert Persson, S. (2006). *Crash-Landing in a Turbulent Transition Market*. Uppsala: Department of Business Studies.

Gebert Persson, S., Steinby, C. (2006). Networks in a protected business context: licenses as restraints and facilitators. *Industrial Marketing Management*, **35**, 870–880.

Ghoshal, S., Bartlett, C.A. (1990). The multinational corporation as an interorganizational network. *Academy of Management Review*, **15**(4), 603–635.

Ghoshal, S., Nohria, N. (1997). *The Differentiated Network. Organizing Multinational Corporations for Value Creation*. San Francisco, CA: Jossey-Bass.

Goodall, K., Roberts, J. (2003). Reprinting managerial knowledge-ability over distance. *Organization Studies*, **24**(7), 1153–1175.

Granovetter, M. (1985). Economic action and social structure: the problem of embeddedness. *American Journal of Sociology*, **91**(3), 481–510.

Håkansson, H. (ed.) (1982). *International Marketing and Purchasing of Industrial Goods. An Interaction Approach*. Chichester: John Wiley & Sons.

Hedlund, G. (1993). Assumptions of hierarchy and heterarchy, with applications to the management of the multinational corporation. In Ghoshal, S., Westney, E. (eds), *Organization Theory and the Multinational Corporation*. London: Macmillan.

Hedlund, G., Rolander, D. (1990). Action in heterarchies: new approaches to managing the MNC. In Bartlett, C., Doz, Y., Hedlund, G. (eds), *Managing the Global Firm*. London: Routledge.

Hennart, J.-F. (1982). *A Theory of Multinational Enterprise*. Ann Arbor, MI: University of Michigan Press.

Hennart, J.-F. (1991). The transaction cost theory of the multinational enterprise. In Pitelis, C.N., Sugden, R. (eds), *The Nature of the Transnational Firm*. London: Routledge.

Hennart, J.-F. (1993). Control in multinational firms: the role of price and hierarchy. In Ghoshal, S., Westney, E. (eds), *Organization Theory and the Multinational Corporation*. New York: St Martin's Press.

Hertz, N. (2003). *The Silent Takeover: Global Capitalism and the Death of Democracy*. New York: Harper Business.

Hickson, D.J., Hinings, C.A., Scheck, L.R.E., Pennings, J.M. (1971). A strategic contingencies theory of intraorganizational power. *Administrative Science Quarterly*, **16**(1), 216–239.

Horaguichi, H., Toyne, T. (1990). Setting the record straight: Hymer, internalization theory and transaction cost economics. *Journal of International Business Studies*, Third Quarter, 487–494.

Hymer, S. (1970). The efficiency (contradictions) of multinational corporations. *American Economic Review*, **60**(2), 411–418.

Hymer, S. (1971). The multinational corporation and the law of uneven development. In Bhagwati, J.W. (ed.), *Economics and World Order*. New York: Macmillan.

Hymer, S. (1972). The internationalization of capital. *Journal of Economic Issues*, **6**(1), 91–111.

Hymer, S. (1976). *The International Operations of National Firms: A Study of Direct Foreign Investments*. Cambridge, MA: MIT Press.

Ietto-Gillies, G. (2012). *Transnational Corporations and International Production*. Cheltenham, UK and Northampton, MA, USA: Edward Elgar.

Johanson, J., Vahlne, J.-E. (1977). The internationalization process of the firm – a model of knowledge development and foreign market commitment. *Journal of International Business Studies*, **1**(1), 83–101.

Johnson, D., Turner, C. (2003). *International Business: Themes and Issues in the Modern Global Economy*. London: Routledge.

Kindleberger, C. (1969). *American Business Abroad*. New Haven, CT: Yale University Press.

Kindleberger, C. (1973). *International Economics*. Homewood, IL: Irwin.

Kirzner, I.M. (1997). Entrepreneurial discovery and the competitive market process: an Austrian approach. *Journal of Economic Literature*, **35**, 60–85.

Kogut, B. (1985). Designing global strategies: profiting from operational flexibility. *Sloan Management Review*, Summer, 15–28.

Kogut, B., Zander, U. (1992). Knowledge of the firm, combinative capabilities and the replication of technology. *Organization Science*, **3**(3), 76–92.

Kogut, B., Zander, U. (1993). Knowledge of the firm and the evolutionary theory of the multinational corporation. *Journal of International Business Studies*, Fourth Quarter, 625–645.

Kogut, B., Zander, U. (1995a). Knowledge and the speed of transfer and imitation of organizational capabilities: an empirical test. *Organization Science*, **6**(1), 76–92.

Kogut, B., Zander, U. (1995b). Knowledge market failure and the multinational enterprise: a reply. *Journal of International Business Studies*, Second Quarter, 417–426.

Kogut, B., Zander, U. (1996). What firms do? Coordination, identity, and learning. *Organization Science*, **7**(5), 502–518.

Kogut, B., Zander, U. (2003). A memoir and reflection: knowledge and an evolutionary theory of the multinational firm ten years later. *Journal of International Business Studies*, **34**, 505–515.

Korten, D.C. (2001). *When Corporations Rule the World*. Bloomfield, CT: Kumarian Press.

Kostova, T. (1999). Organizing legitimacy under conditions of complexity: the case of the multinational enterprise. *Academy of Management Review*, **24**(1), 64–82.

Kostova, T., Zaheer, S. (1999). Organizational legitimacy under conditions of complexity: the case of the multinational enterprise. *Academy of Management Review*, **24**(1), 64–81.

Kutschker, M., Schurig, A. (2002). Embeddedness of subsidiaries in industrial and external networks: a prerequisite for technological change. In Havila, V., Forsgren, M., Håkansson, H. (eds), *Critical Perspectives on Internationalization*. Amsterdam: Pergamon.

Larsson, A. (1985). *Structure and Change. Power in the Transnational Enterprise*. Uppsala: Acta Universitatis Upsaliensis 23.

Lincoln, J.R., Hanada, M., McBride, K. (1986). Organizational structures in Japanese and US manufacturing. *Administrative Science Quarterly*, 31, 338–386.

Madhok, A. (1997). Cost, value and foreign entry mode: the transaction and the firm. *Strategic Management Journal*, 18, 39–61.

Malmberg, A., Sölvell, Ö. (2002). Does foreign ownership matter? Subsidiary impact on local clusters. In Havila, V., Forsgren, M., Håkansson, H. (eds), *Critical Perspectives on Internationalization*. Amsterdam: Pergamon.

Marshall, A. (1890). *Principles of Economics*. London: Macmillan.

Maskell, P., Malmberg, A. (2007). Myopia, knowledge development and cluster evolution. *Journal of Economic Geography*, **7**, 603–618.

McCann, P., Mudambi, R. (2005). Analytical differences in the economics of geography: the case of the multinational firm. *Environment and Planning A*, **47**, 1857–1876.

Nelson, R., Winter, S. (1982). *An Evolutionary Theory of Economic Change*. Cambridge, MA: Harvard University Press.

References                                    187

Ohlin, B. (1967 [1933]). *Interregional and International Trade.* Cambridge, MA: Harvard University Press.

Penrose, E. (1971). *The Large International Firm in Developing Countries. The International Petroleum Industry.* London: Allen & Unwin.

Perrow, C. (1986). *Complex Organizations: A Critical Essay.* New York: Random House.

Pfeffer, J. (1978). *Organizational Design.* Arlington Heights, IL: AHM Publishing Corp.

Polyani, K. (1957). *The Great Transformation.* Boston, MA: Beacon Press.

Porter, M. (1980). *Competitive Strategy: Techniques for Analyzing Industries and Competitors.* New York: Free Press.

Powell, W.W., DiMaggio, P.J. (1991). *The New Institutionalism in Organizational Analysis.* Chicago, IL: University of Chicago Press.

Prahalad, C.K. (2006). *The Fortune at the Bottom of the Pyramid: Eradicating Poverty through Profits.* Upper Saddle River, NJ: Wharton School Publishing.

Prahalad, C.K., Hamel, G. (1990). The core competence of the corporation. *Harvard Business Review,* **90**(3), 79–93.

Richardson, G.B. (1972). The organization of industry. *Economic Journal,* **82**, 883–896.

Rodriguez, P., Siegel, D.S., Hillman, A., Eden, L. (2006). Three lenses on the multinational enterprise: politics, corruption, and corporate social responsibility. *Journal of International Business Studies,* **37**(6), 733–746.

Rosenzweig, P.M., Singh, J.V. (1991). Organizing environments and the multinational enterprise. *Academy of Management Review,* **18**(2), 340–361.

Rugman, A. (1993). Drawing the border for a multinational enterprise and a nation state. In Eden, L., Potter, E. (eds), *Multinational in the Global Political Economy.* New York: St Martin's Press.

Rugman, A. (2003). Regional strategy and the demise of globalization. *Journal of International Management,* **9**, 409–417.

Rugman, A., Verbeke, A. (1998). Multinational enterprises and public policy. *Journal of International Business Studies,* **29**(1), 115–136.

Sahlin-Andersson, K. (2006). Corporate social responsibility: a trend and a movement, but of what and for what? *Corporate Governance,* **6**, 595–608.

Schumpeter, J.A. (1947). *Capitalism, Socialism and Democracy.* New York: Harper.

Scott, W.R. (1981). *Organizations. Rational, Natural, and Open Systems.* Englewood Cliffs, NJ: Prentice Hall.

SOU (1981). De Internationella investeringarnas effecter (The effects of international investments). Stockholm: Gotab.

Stopford, J., Wells, L.T. (1972). *Managing the Multinational Enterprise.* New York: Basic Books.

Szulanski, G. (1995). Unpacking stickiness: an empirical investigation of the barriers to transfer best practise inside the firm. *Academy of Management Journal,* Special Issue, 437–444.

Teece, D.J. (2006). Reflections on the Hymer thesis and the multinational enterprise. *International Business Review,* **15**(2), 124–139.

Teece, D.J., Pisano, G., Shuen, A. (1997). Dynamic capabilities and strategic management. *Strategic Management Journal*, **18**(7), 509–533.
Turnbull, P.W., Valla, J.-P. (1986). *Strategies for International Industrial Marketing*. London: Croom Helm.
van Tulder, R., van der Zwart, A. (2006). *International Business–Society Management: Linking Corporate Responsibility and Globalization*. London: Routledge.
Vernon, R. (1966). International investment in the product cycle. *Quarterly Journal of Economics*, **80**, 190–207.
Westney, E. (1993). Institutionalization theory and the multinational corporation. In Ghoshal, S., Westney, E. (eds), *Organization Theory and the Multinational Corporation*. New York: St Martin's Press.
Williamson, O.E. (1975). *Markets and Hierarchies: Analysis and Antitrust Implications*. New York: Free Press.
World Investment Report (1998). *Trends and Determinants*. New York: United Nations.
World Investment Report (2000). *International Mergers and Acquisitions*. New York: United Nations.
World Investment Report (2005). *Transnational Corporations and the Internationalization of R&D*. New York: United Nations.
World Investment Report (2007). *Transnational Corporations, Extractive Industries and Development*. New York: United Nations.
World Investment Report (2008). *Transnational Corporations and the Infrastructure Change*. New York: United Nations.
World Investment Report (2011). *Non Equity Modes of International Production and Development*. New York: United Nations.
Yamin, M. (1991). A reassessment of Hymer's contribution to the theory of the transnational corporation. In Pitelis, C., Sugden, R. (eds), *The Nature of the Transnational Firm*. London: Routledge.
Yamin, M., Forsgren, M. (2006). Hymer's analysis of the multinational organization: power retention and the demise of the federative MNE. *International Business Review*, **15**(2), 166–179.
Zucker, L. (1983). Organizations as institutions. In Bacharach, S. (ed.), *Research in the Sociology of Organizations*. Greenwich, CT: JAI Press.

# Index